BLOOD-
BOUGHT
WORLD

Published by Canon Press
P.O. Box 8729, Moscow, Idaho 83843
800.488.2034 | www.canonpress.com

Toby J. Sumpter, *Blood-Bought World: Jesus, Idols, and the Bible*
Copyright ©2016 by Toby J. Sumpter

Cover design by James Engerbretson.
Interior detail illustrations by Forrest Dickison.
Interior design by Valerie Anne Bost.

Printed in the United States of America.

Library of Congress Cataloging-in-Publication Data:
Names: Sumpter, Toby, author.
Title: Blood-bought world : Jesus, idols, & the Bible / Toby J. Sumpter.
Description: Moscow : Canon Press, 2016. | Includes bibliographical
   references and index.
Identifiers: LCCN 2016026684 | ISBN 9781591281924 (pbk. : alk.
paper)
Subjects: LCSH: Christianity--Essence, genius, nature. | Jesus
Christ--Person
   and offices. | Christianity and culture.
Classification: LCC BT60 .S85 2016 | DDC 261--dc23
LC record available at https://lccn.loc.gov/2016026684

18 19 20 21 22   10 9 8 7 6 5 4 3

BLOOD-BOUGHT WORLD

JESUS, IDOLS, AND THE BIBLE

Toby J. Sumpter

canonpress
Moscow, Idaho

For my daughter Felicity Elizabeth,
a wise and beautiful woman who lives and loves
like her Savior bought this place

CONTENTS

PART 3: THE MISSION

PREFACE

The journalist Finley Peter Dunne, in the mouth of his fictional character Mr. Dooley, first coined the phrase "comfort the afflicted, afflict the comfortable." In context, he was speaking of the power of newspapers, but the phrase has been picked up and applied to many different causes including, quite understandably, the calling of pastors in the Christian Church. If this book tilts in a particular direction, it tilts toward the latter part of that phrase. Of course the danger with any sort of tilting is the possibility of overbalancing (or overcompensating) and taking a tumble. Martin Luther is remembered for having once said that the "world is like a drunken peasant. If you lift him into the saddle on one side, he will fall off again on the other side. One can't help him no matter how he tries. He wants to be the devil's." So if Luther is right, we don't really need any help leaning. Apparently we're born at a tilt. But if salvation really is a precarious balancing act, ever threatened, always unlikely, or (more truthfully) utterly impossible, I offer this book's "tilt" with a prayer that the Holy Spirit will weave it into His balancing grace.

Since this book leans in the "afflict the comfortable" direction, I want to acknowledge at the outset that I run the risk of afflicting the *afflicted*, or at the very least encouraging people who do. There are many tools in a good pastor's toolbox. Paul told Timothy to "convince, rebuke, exhort, with all long-suffering and teaching" (2 Tim. 4:2). There are different tools for different tasks. This, the book in your hands, is not a tool for every task. But I trust it will be a useful tool for some.

Western civilization as we know it is crumbling, falling in big chunks all around us. The confusions and abominations are growing steadily and increasing rapidly. Meanwhile, there are piles of churches, especially in America, and millions of professing Christians, and yet apparently we are not salt and light. Apparently, we are powerless. We are chased by our enemies. We are fearful of the giants in the land. Which leads me to believe that we are mostly a bunch of Pharisees and scribes and hypocrites. We need a major reformation: we need lots of Christians to become Christians. We need lots of clean-cut, churchgoing folks to meet Jesus in a dark alley and have Him rough them up. It's my prayer that Jesus would be pleased to use this brief offering to that end.

In his book *Against Christianity*, Peter Leithart said, "Contextualization be damned." That quote works as a great three-word summary of his whole book. His thesis is that "Christianity" is a domesticated form of the faith Jesus actually bled and died for. "Christianity" is the neutered version of the vision that Jesus gave to His apostles. "Christianity" is like "religion"—it can be safely studied and handled by professionals with latex gloves behind glass, and the masses are free to think random, vaguely "Christian" thoughts in their heads so long as the thoughts stay there neat and tidy with their shirts tucked in and their hairs all combed. In other words, "Christianity" is neutered and domesticated precisely by being contextualized. If "Christianity" can remain generic, warmed-over thoughts about a deity in the sky, it can be crammed into various philosophies and cultural expressions, like the little girl who dresses up the family bull dog in an Elizabethan bonnet. And inevitably, a neutered "Jesus" gives us piles of little neutered Christians.

But what God has in mind is the complete renovation of the world. Jesus didn't send His apostles out to start a social club, a special interest group, or a new "religion" that could be filed in the yellow pages, right there between Cats and Creeps. Jesus didn't send His apostles out to make deals, to compromise, and offer alternative lifestyles. Jesus claimed *all* authority in heaven and on earth. He claimed all of it, and sent His apostles to announce that claim in the words of the gospel and to enact it with water, bread, and wine, with His full authority. That's what evangelism is: *Hello, World: Jesus bought this place with His blood. Deal with it.* The real faith, once delivered to the saints, is driven by the Spirit of Jesus, a wild, rambunctious, healing force set on the redemption of the world. Men who know this Jesus have no patience for a polite social club with religious jargon.

But this heresy called "Christianity" slips in everywhere. It slips into lots of Reformed Churches who obsess about buzzwords like "gospel" and "gospel-centered" or their pet confessions of faith, and these become mantras and formulas for gatekeeping, shibboleths that justify heresy hunts and rivalry. And some turn to fat theology books and confessions and strain out philosophical gnats in their peer-reviewed journals. Others go for the conference circuit and book signings, and still others measure their holiness by followers on Facebook and retweets on Twitter. And when people get bored with this, there are many places to get new highs with icons and talking to dead people and playing liturgical dress up, while everyone says words like "mystery" and "symbolism" in hushed tones and lots of quotations from old, dead saints.

In other words, too often, "contextualization" is just a buzzword for the sell outs, the insecure Christians who feel the need to pretty-up the gospel. And depending on whom you're whoring after, the gospel gets done up in all kinds of different styles. The academics need lots of footnotes and David Bentley Hart vocabulary so that they can feel deep and profound. Others need rock music and strobe lights and screens and tattoos. And still others need relics and icons and bearded men with fancy hats. But Jesus isn't making any deals. Jesus doesn't want a place at the table of coolness. Jesus isn't trying to get His voice to be heard. His voice is what holds the whole universe up. His Word is what commanded this world into existence. It's only His mercy that keeps our atoms from flying apart.

"Contextualization be damned" because Jesus comes with the life of God for the world, and the world is dead and dying and demon infested. You don't contextualize life for dead people. What good would that do? Does it really matter what Jesus was wearing when He got to the grave of Lazarus? Would Lazarus have been a little more reluctant if Jesus was wearing His blue tunic or led the crowd in singing a traditional hymn? Jesus came to establish His Kingdom, His culture, His life in this world. Our job is to deal with it.

And this is the thing: Jesus *has* succeeded. He has been conquering this world by His Word and Spirit these last two thousand years. And that's why we have cool things like theology books and confessions of faith and liturgies and hymns. And because we're human, there is always *that* context. It's inescapable. We always come into the middle of a conversation. We are born into the middle of a conversation. Our stories wake up in the middle of the Great Story. And no one can object to that reality. What *Jesus* objects to is allowing any of His gifts to be used as leashes on the Spirit or His people. Jesus refuses to be domesticated.

So on the spectrum of traditional and contemporary, I'm way over on the traditional side (even though there's a southern California hippie deep inside my soul). But that means that the dangers I (and my people) face are the temptations of turning the Conquest of Jesus into a formula with old prayers, rituals, and a tidy liturgy. That's "Christianity," and we're against that.

So what do we do? Where do we turn? We turn to Jesus. We cry out to our Savior, our God, our King. We ask Him to save us from ourselves, to save us from all our programs, all our fads, all our theologizing, and we ask Him to pour out the Holy Spirit on us. But we don't need some kind of cheap spray-on revival. We don't need some kind of dress-up, some kind of toupee of holiness. The Church is already full of enough clowns and cowards. We need the Holy Spirit to come and raise us from the dead. We need Jesus to breathe His life into us. And when this happens it will be unmistakable, because it will make lots of people really mad. It will turn the world upside again, like it did the Roman Empire centuries ago. And for the first time in a long time, we will hear men preaching all of Jesus, all of the Bible, and, for a change, they will speak clearly into the microphone, and people will actually listen because they have met the real Jesus. They won't sell out for anyone, because now they have backbones.

When people know the real Jesus they become real men and real women—really human—and that makes them bold, creative, fearless, compassionate, and glad. When people know Jesus, they know they have nothing to lose, nothing to fear, and the world is before them. And Jesus sends them out with His blessing to discover, invent, create, rule, bless, heal, explore, and die with smiles on their faces, because they know the Man who is truly Alive, and now they can't stay dead anymore.

READING THE STORY
WRONG

It has been pointed out that one of the greatest failures of every attempt to dramatize the gospels has been their complete inability to capture how Jesus could elicit such intense, visceral hatred to the point of mob justice, incited by the Jewish religious leaders and a troop of complicit Romans. No Jesus-actor has ever captured this. They are all too nice and too soft spoken, and even in their rare angry moments they seem utterly nonthreatening, barely copping an effeminate whine. If we are paying attention to these dramatizations, it's almost impossible to sympathize with the

Jewish leaders, with the crowds calling for His blood, with the difficulty of Pilate's political plight. For all our professed love of story arc and depth of character, we are left with a one-dimensional Jesus and flat, simplistic bad guys. We are left with narrative tautologies. They do bad things because they are bad guys. Jesus does good things because He is good.

But this is not merely a failure of imagination; this is a failure of exegesis, a failure to read the story carefully. And this has had (and continues to have) disastrous results in the Christian Church. What is there to imitate in such a Jesus? What is there to avoid in such Pharisees? Faithful imitation is impossible because we cannot imitate a cardboard cutout of God (not to mention the Christological heresies involved). And faithful denunciation is impossible because we cannot imagine such folly actually showing up in the real world. We are training ourselves to identify bad guys by their labels and uniforms—probably dressed up like Jewish High Priests in turbans or Roman Governors bedecked with olive-leaf crowns and everything. Anything short of a Halloween spectacle, and people immediately start tsk-tsking you for being so judgmental. *How can you know their hearts?* And feelings get hurt.

But it's not just the Savior that we read poorly—though that is the center of the problem. We do the same with Paul and Peter. And with Moses and David. Perhaps we are a bit better with the Old Testament heroes. But because of our simplistic reading of Jesus, we still force everything into rigid moralistic categories, tending to opt for the when-in-doubt-remember-they-aren't-perfect option. And so we have something of a binary switch to flip off and on with our Sunday School flannel graph presentations. *David killing the giant = good. David committing adultery with Bathsheba = bad.* And sure, that's right as far as it goes, but we have no categories for Rahab's righteous deception, for Gideon's godly vandalism, and for the countless breaches of decorum found in the prophets.

Don't misunderstand: this is no trendy call for narrative relativism. In fact, I sort of flinch every time I hear words like "story" and "narrative" these days. I start bracing for the vanilla-latte sellout, complete with stylish glasses and a Madonna mic. Usually it starts with edgy exegetical points making fun of fundamentalists and literalism, and ends up with a book deal, a feature in *O! Magazine*, and eventually saying a blessing over the nuptials of a guy who wants to have sex with his poodle.

There are all kinds of problems with that, but here is the point I want to make in this book: there were about fifty steps in front of the exegetical gymnastics that led to the poodle abuse in which all the sharp edges and pointy parts of Scripture were explained away, watered down, and functionally deleted. In other words, a dramatic failure to read the actual *story*. We only hear what we wanted hear, what we expected to hear, what we assume the authors meant to say.

And plenty of *well-meaning* Christians contribute to this problem. They do it with their don't-try-this-at-home exegesis of Scripture. But they also do it by reading the Bible in such a way as to cover the whole thing in a clear preservative lacquer that leaves nothing to try at home even if we wanted to. All we are left with are a number of unimaginable bad examples and a few Precious Moments poses, hands pressed together, gazing longingly into heaven, with angels lisping and prancing in the background. These well-meaning Christians are (unintentionally) holier than God, and they leave us unarmed, unprepared, and ill equipped for the real world.

Of course it's totally hip to give fundamentalists the finger these days, and at the end of the day, we have to say that they were simply wonderful in some ways and completely awful in others. Forced to choose between the fundies and the liberals, we should choose to be a fundy going to heaven any day over a liberal who'll make good kindling on the last day. But a good illustration of the "Precious Moments" problem is the whole prohibitionist movement that co-opted many sectors of the Church for decades.

Honestly, I'm somewhat afraid that the return of dark beer and other alcohol to the Church may not necessarily be any more momentous than rock bands and strobe lights in many modern worship services, which is to say, only indicative of another line of compromise. Now our Christian frat boys can get tipsy like the world too . . . But be that as it may, the Bible does teach that God gave wine to make our hearts glad. Jesus turned water into wine, not Welch's grape juice. And at the Last Supper, Jesus commanded His disciples to celebrate a particular meal until the end of the world—and that meal includes sharing real, dangerous wine. The Bible clearly teaches that wine is dangerous. Wine is a mocker. Wine may deceive. The drunkard and the glutton and the sluggard are three friends with a similar sad fate. But the fact remains that Jesus gave us wine *because* wine is a fiery drink—a spirit that reminds us of the Holy Spirit, dangerous and powerful. In other words, God gives His people dangerous things like wine, and the Word of God, which is the sword of the Spirit.

If the Church in the West is to recover from its current stupor, we need once again to be filled with the fire of the Holy Ghost. We need to unsheathe the sword of the Spirit. Usually, in whiskey making, the whiskey is watered down when bottled, sometimes for taste, sometimes to meet regulations. The actual alcohol content of the whiskey in its cask varies but is known as "cask strength" or "barrel proof," referring to the natural intensity of the whiskey coming straight out of the barrel. We need the undiluted intensity of the gospel to burn our throats and kick us in the gut. We need a barrel-proof gospel. We need to let the sharp edges of Scripture cut us. We need to let the actual words, the actual story, the actual characters, confront us, shape us, scare us, repulse us. If the Church is to rise up again full of preachers, missionaries, evangelists, men who don't give a damn about the fleeting pleasures of this life, and care only for the glory of Jesus and His Kingdom, we must once again see Jesus, know Jesus, and grasp what made Him so eminently *killable*. Because I'm afraid that until crosses fill the nations of the West, until we once again embody the threat that Jesus and His disciples so clearly were, there will continue to be only superficial conversions and a cultural "Christianity" that constantly sells out to the latest fads and trends.

At the moment we are inundated with idols. Idols are what the descendants of Adam make out of their fears. Idols are Fear Incarnate. Nothings made of metal, stone, wood, and paint. And then, because of the gravity inherent in the world that God made, those who serve the images become like them. Instead of fixing our eyes on Jesus, instead hearing His word and becoming like Him, our vision grows dim and our hearing dull, and we become like the lifeless icons we kiss and fondle.

This book consists of three parts. The first part illustrates the offense of the gospel, the sharp edges of Jesus and His favorite men. The second part describes various ways we try to hide from this real Jesus and craft idols to protect ourselves from the full force of His claims. And finally, the third part turns to the duty of obedience in faith, in worship, in mission, in work, in the Church, and in our homes and families.

In the meantime, we cannot be surprised that the Church embodies its Jesus-actors so well. The best Christ-imitators ought to be our pastors, our elders, our leaders, our men, but what are they imitating? Are they imitating a Jesus who would threaten anyone anywhere? Or are they imitating a Jesus who said vague, pious sounding aphorisms and performed random, benevolent magic tricks to impress the media? We tend to make men who are either overly emotional or overly intellectual, but the center of a man, the center of his courage, of his virtue, of his faithfulness was meant to be his chest. As C.S. Lewis prophetically noted decades ago, "In a sort of ghastly simplicity we remove the organ and demand the function. We make men without chests and expect of them virtue and enterprise. We laugh at honour and are shocked to find traitors in our midst. We castrate and bid the geldings be fruitful."

May Jesus be kind and once again give us men with chests.

PART 1

LEAVING SHARP EDGES SHARP

C H A P T E R   1

ANGER WITHOUT SIN

The introduction on the previous pages runs the
risk of sounding alarmist or like a lot of bluster.
And that is the tack many men take when they are
unable to actually lead. Instead of doing the hard,
sacrificial work of explaining the truth, serving the
weak, and standing there cheerful, immovable, always abounding in the work of the Lord, they turn
up the volume and get mad. It has the appearance
of strength, often starts fights, and occasionally gets
a little bit done. Young bucks are particularly suscep-
tible to the allure of wrath. The problem is that the
long-term results are uniformly disappointing and

disastrous. "A wrathful man stirreth up strife: but he that is slow to anger appeaseth strife" (Prov. 15:18). Elsewhere Proverbs says that an angry man not only stirs up strife but ends up in trouble constantly. And the moment you bail him out, he's back at it five minutes later like a dog on a bone (Prov. 19:19).

But the gospels are not shy about recording the fact that Jesus frequently stirred up strife. Occasionally, Jesus even acted in anger: "And when he had looked round about them with anger, being grieved for the hardness of their hearts, he saith unto the man, stretch forth thine hand. And he stretched it out: and his hand was restored whole as the other. And the Pharisees went forth, and straightway took counsel with the Herodians against him, how they might destroy him" (Mk. 3:5–6). We need to learn how to get into trouble like Jesus.

The text clearly says that Jesus was angry, and then the Pharisees went out and plotted with the Herodians. If you can't imagine the media frenzy, then you aren't reading your Bible rightly. If you can't imagine the concerned conversations, the puzzled posts on Facebook, the hand-wringing emails that hit His inbox that afternoon, you aren't paying attention. *Jesus, you really should be more careful, more mindful of your audience, more tactful, more aware of how some people might misinterpret you.* Even His friends might be concerned. *Might there not be a more sensitive way to approach things with the Pharisees?*

Too often we read our Bibles like they are fairy tales and comic books, with all the good guys and bad guys clearly labeled, missing the complexities in the story—the complexities that would actually require us to grow up into wisdom.

The Bible confronts us with the difference between the wrath and bluster of the flesh and the fierce boldness of the Spirit that rested on Jesus. When we talk about the real Jesus, the One who made people around Him mad with some regularity, we know we are not talking about a man with anger management issues. We know that Jesus didn't stir up strife because He was a wrathful man. Jesus never flew off the handle. And we know that no disciple of His may either. Paul says explicitly that the leaders of the church must be self-controlled, gentle, temperate, and not quick-tempered or violent (1 Tim. 3:2–3, Tit. 1:7–8). James also insists: "Wherefore, my beloved brethren, let every man be swift to hear, slow to speak, slow to wrath: for the wrath of man worketh not the righteousness of God" (Jas. 1:19–20). And Paul again: "Be ye angry, and sin not: let not the sun go down upon your wrath; neither give place to the devil" (Eph. 4:26–27).

So how are we to distinguish between the kind of trouble Jesus was constantly in and the kind of trouble angry men find themselves in? What is the difference between the righteous anger of Jesus and the wrath of man that only stirs up strife and the devil? And just to make matters more complicated, let's not forget to point out that plenty of angry men, who deserve every ounce of trouble they bring upon themselves, will be the first to point out they are just victims of their circumstances, *like Jesus*, suffering for righteousness' sake.

This is why it is not enough to merely assert the difference. We must not merely repeat our tautologies. *Good guys do good things; bad guys do bad things.* This is only to beg the question, and in the end we're left to the tyranny of popular opinion. If you get enough complaints, if there's enough offense taken, if respected leaders hint you were less than tactful, then you should probably apologize, probably take the post down, probably just stick to happy texts in your preaching.

Or worse, the reply comes back *Jesus was God, and you're not Jesus*. Right. Agreed. But this Jesus is our

Master, our Teacher, and we must imitate Him, or we will imitate an idol. In Him is life, and we will have nothing else. It is no longer we who live but rather Christ who lives in us. We must not be wrathful, divisive men; we must not be blustering, foolish men. But we must have Jesus. We must have *this* Jesus, the real Jesus, or we will die. Wisdom demands that we stand on this precipice, that we feel this danger, that we take this risk. We must learn this Jesus or else we will continue to find ourselves retreating on every cultural battlefield. If we don't understand in our bones the difference between Christ-like troublemaking and fleshly pride and bluster, then we will only be left with cowards and fools. On the one hand, we will continue to have good men constantly second guessing, afraid of stirring up strife, apologizing for speaking the truth, caving to the pressures of popular opinion for acting like the real Jesus and hurting feelings. And on the other hand, in place of these "good" cowards, we will have the undisciplined ravings of a few who see the insanity but do not know what spirit they are of, men who constantly undermine the mission of the Kingdom with their destructive outbursts.

For all the times Jesus caused men's blood to boil, we must learn that, just as often, His refusal to fight fire with fire was used by God to *appease* strife. As He would say at different points in His own ministry: He came to bring peace on earth (Jn. 14:27, 16:33, cf. Acts 10:36). But not only did Jesus say that He came to bring peace, He also said that did *not* come to bring peace, but a sword and division (Mt. 10:34–39, Luke 12:51–53). I suspect that the answer to our question lies somewhere in the matrix of this dual reality. Jesus came to bring peace *and* Jesus did not come to bring peace. This is no contradiction, but it represents the challenge of reading the gospels honestly and carefully. This is the real Jesus, the Jesus we must know and love and imitate.

In the Sermon on the Mount, Jesus gives us a hint regarding the answer to this tension. He blesses the peacemakers as children of God and immediately addresses those persecuted for righteousness' sake, those reviled and lied about (Mt. 5:9–11). So one way of harmonizing what Jesus says is by noticing that the kind of peacemaking Jesus and His followers are pursuing always infuriates certain kinds of people. The *peace* that accompanies true justice gets reviled and lied about. We need to get our minds around the fact that this peace and justice will not float down out of heaven with a golden glow and an emotional soundtrack playing in the background. This peace and justice will come wrapped in real time, in personalities, in the complexities of people in history. It's relatively easy to offer mental assent to the idea of following Jesus to the point of losing family and offending friends, but when it comes right down to it, people are rarely ready.

Consider the time Jesus healed the demoniac who was raving mad among the tombs. In order to understand what follows, it is necessary to begin to grasp the gravity of what Jesus does in releasing the demons named "legion" (Mk. 5:9) into the swine, numbering about two thousand, which then run violently down the steep place into the sea and drown (Mt. 8:32, Mk. 5:13). Remember that pigs were an unclean animal for Jews but considered sacred by the Greeks and Romans. Here, in the country of the Gadarenes, Hellenism has infiltrated the culture. Decapolis apparently denotes a community of ten cities, and such an enormous herd of pigs suggests the presence of at least a pagan temple or two. Consider the economic loss involved in this act of healing. It's likely that there would be enormous repercussions for this event. How many people got fired that day? How many men went home without a paycheck? Who took the loss? Were there debts? Did some children go hungry? Was anyone evicted? What about the environmental repercussions? I don't know what two thousand pig carcasses do to a body of water, but that ecosystem was bound to be a bit out of balance for a while. Who spent days dredging the Sea of Galilee? Or did that beach just have an awful stench for months? Did Jesus do any restitution? Was He planning to go turn Himself into the authorities before the people begged Him to leave (Mt. 8:34)? Mark says that they were *afraid* when they saw the demoniac clothed and in his right mind and heard what Jesus had done (Mk. 5:15–18). Were some of the disciples afraid too? Would *you* have been afraid?

What had Jesus done? Why pick a fight with the Romans, with the businessmen, with the religious and cultural leaders, with the common folk of those cities? Wouldn't it attract all the wrong kind of attention? First off, you're going to get mistaken for a revolutionary extremist. The Zealots are going to come out of the hills with their pitchforks in about ten minutes assuming you're their new leader. Second, the Romans will peg you as a revolutionary, and word is going to get back to Jerusalem. Everything will be scrutinized. Now there will be trouble. Now there will be anger and strife. Is this really what "seeking the peace of the city" looks like?

But there in the midst of the rubble, in the midst of the fear, a sudden, wonderful peace *has* descended. A man is sitting clothed and in his right mind. That's what salvation is. We are all born in sin, infected with the madness of guilt, enslaved to Satan and his armies, living among the tombs, tormented by death until Jesus orders the demons to leave. Then we are clothed in the glory and righteousness of Jesus. Like the words of the old hymn: *Jesus, Thy blood and righteousness my beauty are; my glorious dress.* Sitting and clothed in his right mind—this is the unmistakable peace of salvation.

There is more to say, but let's begin with this: There is an anger that is not wrathful bluster. There is a peace that causes division. There is a righteousness that incites lies and mockery and upheaval *and doesn't care*. World, meet the real Jesus.

CHAPTER 2

THE AUTHORITY OF THE AUTHOR

To tell stories is to assert authority. This is what an author is. An author invokes the right to tell you a narrative, to describe a scene, and to arrange the details in a particular order from a particular point of view. And this is central to what made Jesus so hated, so resented, and so envied. It was His authoritative, *authorial* voice.

"And when he was come into the temple, the chief priests and the elders of the people came unto him as he was teaching, and said, by what authority doest thou these things? And who gave thee this authority?"

(Mt. 21:23, cf. Mk. 11:28) The people were particularly astonished at the teaching of Jesus because His word was with authority (Lk. 4:32). And when He cast out a demon, they were all amazed, "for with authority and power he commandeth the unclean spirits, and they come out" (Lk. 4:36). When Jesus sent His disciples out to begin their ministry, it was with this same authority: "Then he called his twelve disciples together, and gave them power and authority over all devils, and to cure diseases. And he sent them to preach the kingdom of God, and to heal the sick" (Lk. 9:1–2). Likewise, when the seventy returned from their mission, He said, "Behold, I give unto you power to tread on serpents and scorpions, and over all the power of the enemy: and nothing shall by any means hurt you" (Lk. 10:19). In the same spirit, after the resurrection, Jesus claims that all authority in heaven and on earth has been given to Him, and on that basis sends the apostles to make disciples of all nations (Mt. 28:18–19).

On the one hand, we spill countless pages of ink on the downstream details in these descriptions. Should we expect to regularly perform exorcisms in our church services? What about the snake handlers and other Christian showbiz performers? What about the charismatic gifts? What about the presence of demons and evil spirits? I grant that the Church needs to answer these questions, but in the midst of the clamor we miss the most obvious part: Whatever the role of demons, whatever the place of exorcisms, whatever the regularity of miracles, the common thread holding the ministry of Jesus and His disciples together is His *authority*.

And though it is clear that the authority of Jesus extended to evil powers, sickness, death, and even the natural elements, it was His *teaching* that really amazed people, shocked some, and enraged others. And the centerpiece of His teaching was a kind of storytelling, a way of naming characters and events that pried hearts open with the crowbar of the Spirit. His stories claimed authority, and He sent His disciples out with the same authority.

But we have lost this authority. Somehow we have even grown accustomed to it, and somehow it is not much of a threat to anyone, especially here in the West. When we tell stories, our stories make no authoritative claims. At best we repeat eternal truths that do not touch down in this world, that do not confront, that do not challenge. And at worst, we tell stories that primarily submit themselves to the narrative of the world. We let the political and cultural gods of our age dictate the key terms and legislate morality. Rather than subverting these claims, we dutifully submit to this alien authority. If the world says that there's an overpopulation problem, we bow our heads and nod obediently. If they say you have to recycle or else you hate creation and your grandchildren, we cower and rush to separate our trash. If they say organic is holy, we cross ourselves twice and check all the labels three times.

Yes, Jesus came as the embodiment of God. But He was also fully man, the embodiment of Israel, the new Adam for every failed Adam. He came to be what Israel was always meant to be, what every son of Adam was born to be: an authoritative representation of God, His image bearer, His spokesman, His son. The stories that Jesus told and the story that He embodied took up the entire Old Testament narrative of Israel, the covenant promises to Abraham and David for the whole world, and then plunked it all down in first century Palestine, naming names and calling names. Jesus dared to interpret the story. He dared to connect dots from salvation history to the present day. Not only was Jesus God Incarnate, Emmanuel—God with us, Jesus was God's authoritative Word, the eternal Logos, particularized at a particular point in time, in a particular place. This is the great offense.

To claim this authority, to dare as a mere human to interpret the world, history, current events is to look and seem like a megalomaniac, like an arrogant power-tripper. *Who do you think you are? Who died and left you king?* Well, as it turns out, Jesus did. We are sons and daughters of the God who made this place. We are His friends, and we have been authorized to speak on His behalf. We do not speak on our own authority; we are just people made of dust. But the Eternal Son died and rose again, and has left His Spirit here, making us kings and priests to our God. We must not take ourselves too seriously, but we have been given the authority of the Author Himself.

Jesus sent the seventy, and He still sends the faithful, as sheep among wolves (Lk. 10:3). It is no threat to anyone anywhere to announce generic news, generic information. But to assert particulars is to assert authority. To proclaim the Kingdom of Heaven here and now is to proclaim the authority of Jesus here and now. To assert that a particular cultural expression is folly, a particular political event is rebellion, or a particular person is a blasphemer is to assert authorial power, the right to tell the story, the right to interpret the facts on the ground. This works with straightforward naming, but it is also embedded in irony, mockery, and jokes. To make light of something is an insult to some (blasphemy) and a kindly gesture to others (deliverance). And the more particular you are, the more limited you necessarily are. But this is the risk of the Incarnation, the risk of authority incarnate.

Assigning names and roles or evaluating fruit and brambles frequently does not appear to account for the complexities of the world. To claim that a man's tight jeans and gelled and frosted hair is a sacrifice of praise to his metrosexual goddess of deviance doesn't take into account all the potential exceptions. *Can you see his heart? Do you know what kind of family he grew up in? Could that just be his own personal style, completely innocent, completely Christ honoring?* Yes, it is possible. There is nothing innately moral about the tightness of your trousers or how you comb your hair. "Who art thou that judgest another man's servant? To his own master he standeth or falleth" (Rom. 14:4). Or what if a pastor waves a warning flag, pointing out that the same "alternative health" evangelists are often pro-abortion and pro-sodomy? In other words, what if they don't have a great track record for making crucial distinctions? If they can't tell the difference between a lump of tissue and a human being, if they aren't sure how sexual intercourse was designed to work, why would you trust them to help you with ear infections or give you advice about magical healing oils? And even as I raise these particular examples, exceptions leap to your mind. *Isn't it kind of insulting to associate homeopathic medicine with sodomy? Don't you know that there are conscientious Christians making careful distinctions who are pro-life, stand for biblical sexuality, and find essential oils extremely helpful?* Yes, I realize that. But Jesus faced the same challenges. He called the Pharisees hypocrites and snakes, and there were some Pharisees who weren't. He mocked their tithing, their vestments, their prayers, and their oaths, and surely there were some Pharisees who participated in some measure in all of these things with true faith before God.

This is what authority does. It names, it narrates, and it points to the end of the story. It generalizes, it links motifs, it assigns typologies, and it presses them to a sharp point. Jesus rides a white horse, and He marches on this world in righteousness, judging and making war (Rev. 19:11). His name is called The Word of God, and out of His mouth goes a sharp sword, that He might strike all the nations of the earth (Rev. 19:13–15). For He must reign until He has put all of His enemies under His feet (1 Cor. 15:25). But we have exchanged this Jesus for an impostor with a Nerf gun. He rides a repurposed ten-speed to limit his carbon footprint, eats free-range chickens because of an article he read one time on the internet, and tries really hard to buy his coffee beans from fair trade sources because the girl behind the counter shows a lot of cleavage.

Of course it's been the postmodern fashion to play with these themes. All language is inherently violent and coercive, we are told, and therefore all we can do is expose the power plays and attempt to keep a balance of powers by writing over-corrective histories of minority positions. All very schizophrenic if you buy the whole survival of the fittest theory. Why not let nature take its course? Why not let the strong dominate? And of course we might question the point of even caring, but that takes us even further afield.

But before Foucault and Derrida were wetting their beds in fear of linguistic oppression, the Bible already told us that words were powerful. God's Word created the worlds. Life and death are in the power of the tongue. Good words are health to the body, while others are rottenness to the bones. The tongue is a wild fire able to do great harm, setting whole worlds ablaze.

And yet Jesus still sends people out to preach, to teach, to talk, to sing, to write, to exhort, to correct, to testify. And there is a fleshly authority that Jesus warns His followers about: "The kings of the Gentiles exercise lordship over them; and they that exercise authority upon them are called benefactors. But ye shall not be so: but he that is greatest among you, let him be as the younger; and he that is chief, as he that doth serve" (Lk. 22:25–26).

And so there we are, left with an explosive power in our mouths and yet sent out to speak as servants of Christ and not Gentile lords. Moses was a *servant* when he walked into Pharaoh's court. Elijah was a *servant* when he mocked Baal and his prophets on Mount Carmel. John was a *servant* when he told Herod that he ought not have his brother's wife. And Jesus was a *servant* when He overturned the tables in the temple and drove out the sellers with a whip. Sometimes servants stand and wait. Sometimes servants are silent. Sometimes servants do not answer the fools. And sometimes they do.

We must be careful. We must beware. We have not been sent out to destroy men's lives, but that they might have life. But let there be no mistake: If we open our mouths and speak with the authority of the

King of Kings, if we actually apply the Word of God to all of life, if we dare speak on behalf of God, we will be questioned. We will be misinterpreted. We will be misunderstood. But we have been sent not to be served, but to serve and to give our lives gladly for the healing and salvation of many.

CHAPTER 3

PARABOLIC MINISTRY

Despite all the cheap, postmodern knock-offs, parable and story really are crucial to understanding the Bible, Jesus, and what it means to be His Church in this world. If we want to know Jesus, if we want to imitate Him, we need to read His story well. And as it turns out, central to understanding *His* story is listening carefully to the stories that He told. Not only did Jesus tell parables, but the life of Jesus is itself a parable, a riddle, a challenge, an authoritative confrontation.

N.T. Wright has pointed out that the parables of Jesus were not merely stories with information to be considered, they were prophetic announcements that demanded a response. Jesus came announcing that the story of Israel and her God was coming to a climax in Him. The Kingdom of God was at hand, arriving in their midst. The actions and stories of Jesus *are* that Kingdom coming. And the only responses possible are faith or unbelief—following the One who claims to be the Messiah or rejecting Him.

We see this in Mark's gospel where the healing of the demoniac comes immediately on the heels of Jesus calming the storm (Mk. 4:35–41). Jesus speaks to the wind and the waves and says, "Peace, be still!" And the disciples are afraid: "Who can this be, that even the wind and the sea obey Him?" And as soon as they come to the other side of the sea, another storm meets them: a man infested with a squall of demons. This was a storm no man could calm—he had often been chained and shackled, but he had pulled the chains and shackles apart again and again. Once again, Jesus speaks the word: peace. And the storm obeys Him, and the man is healed.

But before the demoniac—just before He calmed the stormy sea—Jesus explained what His ministry was all about: "And he taught them many things by parables . . . " (Mk. 4:2). As Mark introduces the parables of Jesus, he spends a curious amount of space setting the scene: "And he began to teach by the sea side: and there was gathered unto him a great multitude, so that he entered into a ship, and sat in the sea; and the whole multitude was by the sea on the land" (Mk. 4:1). Given the significant role the "sea" will play as the chapter goes on, it hardly seems accidental that Mark, who is otherwise sparse with detail, underlines the fact that Jesus is teaching from a boat *in the sea*. This is not merely a practical solution to the crowd, it demonstrates something about what Jesus is doing while He tells parables. He is riding in the sea. He is fishing. He is measuring depths. He's taking His disciples into stormy gales.

The first parable from the boat is the parable of the sower. The seed is the word of God, and the word of God is received or rejected in a number of different ways. Satan takes the word away from some hearts (Mk. 4:15). In others, it takes no root, and the afflictions and persecution offend them (v. 17). Still others hear the word, but riches and lusts choke it and it becomes unfruitful (v. 19). Finally are those who hear the word, receive it, and bring forth fruit (v. 20). And Jesus says that *this parable* is the key to understanding all the parables: "And he said unto them, Know ye not this parable? And how then will ye know all parables?" (v. 13).

Part of the point is related to the nature of knowing and perceiving the truth. "And he said unto them, he that hath ears to hear, let him hear . . . Unto you it is given to know the mystery of the kingdom of God: but unto them that are without, all these things are done in parables: that seeing they may see, and not perceive; and hearing they may hear, and not understand; lest at any time they should be converted, and their sins should be forgiven them . . . and with many such parables spake he the word unto them, as they were able to hear it. But without a parable spake he not unto them . . . " (Mk. 4:9, 11–12, 33–34). Jesus says knowledge of the kingdom is found in Him, but to everyone else, it's all parables, all mystery, all dark and muffled and confusing. Mark says Jesus only speaks in riddles. This is because the kingdom of God is a *mystery*. Jesus has come to bring peace, but His peace is startling, terrifying, confusing, and causes upheaval. Parables are not biblical fairy tales—stories to make people smile and nod off to sleep. Parables are not morality plays or cautionary tales, carefully calculated to get people to act in certain ways or avoid certain behavior. Parables are dark sayings, riddles, storms in the midst of the sea, that cause grown men to fear and tremble. Parables probe hearts and test minds. They demand to know what you're made of. And this is why parables often made people mad. They reveal cowards and traitors and compromisers, and nobody likes to be naked in the spotlight.

The obvious question that arises from the parable of the sower is *Which one am I?* Jesus is saying that mere acquaintance with the word is not sufficient. Lots of word falls on deaf ears and hard hearts, and there are even some who receive it momentarily but ultimately reject it. The implication is clear: Jesus is warning the Jews that they are in danger of being various forms of bad soil. They are the chosen people of God. They are the covenant people. They have the law. They have the Sabbath. They pray and fast. And Jesus says: *so what.*

But Jesus is saying more than this. He's announcing that *His Word* is the word being sown. *He* is the word come into the soil of Israel, and only those who hear and receive *Him* will be fruitful. All of His parables are represented in this one parable of the sower (Mk. 4:13). All of His parables are the word being sown, and all of the parables are revealing hearts made of stone, hearts held captive by Satan, and hearts infested with thorns—*by how they respond to Him*. And only those who follow Jesus get answers. Only those who follow Him into the house, only those who demand an answer, an explanation—only those are the ones who get one: "But without a parable spake he not unto them: and when they were alone, he expounded all things to his disciples" (Mk. 4:34). He only speaks in parables, and He only explains what He means when they are alone (Mk. 4:10–11). These are the good ground, those who follow after Jesus with questions.

But we hear these summaries and smile and nod and shrug our shoulders blankly. We imagine Jesus in a Pantene Pro-V commercial floating across the room, light glinting off his blonde locks while He speaks in soothing tones. We don't hear the judgment in His voice. We don't hear the warning. We don't get the confusion. But Jesus says, "all these things are done in parables: that seeing they may see, and not perceive; and hearing they may hear, and not understand; lest at any time they should be converted, and their sins should be forgiven them" (Mk. 4:11–12). Jesus says He's telling parables because Israel is under a curse. Parables are announcements of God's judgment. Jesus told parables so that some people *wouldn't* repent. Jesus told parables so that some people would not see, not hear, and not understand. Jesus says He tells stories so that some people will go to Hell. Listen to what Matthew says, "And when the chief priests and Pharisees had heard his parables, they perceived that he spake of them. But when they sought to lay hands on him, they feared the multitude, because they took him for a prophet" (Mt. 21:45–46). The chief priests and Pharisees understood Jesus. They knew He was talking about them. They knew He was cursing them. And then, lost and blind in their sins, people got mad. This is why when Jesus told parables, sometimes the nice religious people wanted to *kill* him.

It is so easy to hear Jesus only filtered through our pristine theological categories: *He's God. He's always right. He's perfect. He knows everything.* But this is to side-step the full gut-punch of the Word. Hear the Word spoken by a young pastor in His early thirties. Listen to Him tell stories to trained theologians that confuse them. Isn't that a little disrespectful? Isn't that arrogant? Isn't He being obnoxious? And why launch into such a judgmental sermon series? He seems to be suggesting that lots of His listeners are compromised, at odds with God, even tools of Satan. It's extreme, over the top, sensationalist. And notice all the followers He's gathering around Him. Notice how everyone is talking about Him. He's a young celebrity pastor with thousands of followers clearly critiquing the establishment. *This is not just inconvenient. This is dangerous. This could ruin everything.*

In this sense, the life of Jesus is a riddle, a parable, a dark saying. He is the God of Israel come to His own, but He's come incognito. He's come wrapped in mysterious words, dark humility, and a childish audacity. He comes telling stories of judgment. He comes intentionally confusing people. He comes cursing. Nowhere is this more pointed than in the parable of the cross. The cross is a cursed death. The cross is a symbol of shame. The cross is a symbol of failure and subjugation to Roman rule. The cross is weakness, guilt, and defeat. And Jesus says if any man come after Me, let him take up his cross and follow Me. The parables are a curse pronounced on Israel, and the cross is that parable-curse taken *for* Israel.

What kind of homiletics training is this? I doubt there is a preaching class in existence that encourages telling offensive parables as the centerpiece of one's pulpit ministry. The instructor of such a class would say something like: *You can tell if you did a good job by how many questions you get after the message. Expect two or three good controversies each decade. The more follow-up notes asking for clarification, the better. Get run out of town at least once. Get called names. Receive anonymous death threats.*

Paul says to imitate him as he imitates Christ: beaten, stoned, chased out of town, hungry, misunderstood, rejected, shipwrecked (cf. 2 Cor. 11:23–30). Paul says that's how you know he's a real apostle. That's his résumé, the proof his gospel is authentic. Paul has battle scars to prove it. The word of God is "quick and powerful, and shaper than any two-edged sword, piercing even to the dividing asunder of soul and spirit, and of the joints and marrow, and is a discerner of the thoughts and intents of the heart" (Heb. 4:12). Those who wield that sword should bear the marks of the cross in their bodies. But modern preaching is a lot of posturing and people-pleasing.

The point is *not* to stand up and try to offend and confuse everybody. Parabolic preaching is not doing your best James Joyce impression with Bible words, neither is it some kind of Yosemite Sam rant. Wisdom is justified by her children. What are the results of Jesus' ministry? A man with a withered hand restored. A man sitting clothed and in his right mind, a storm calmed and at peace, demons scattered, a man joyfully proclaiming his salvation, disciples producing fruit, some thirtyfold, some sixty, and some a hundred. This is a parabolic ministry: a ministry that confronts, offends, terrifies, bewilders, and heals with the grace and truth of Jesus.

CHAPTER 4

FIGHTING
LIKE A PROPHET

These days, articles and books bemoaning conflict in the Church and the "culture wars" are ubiquitous. And with the rise of social media, we all know a lot more about many of the flash points than previously in Church history. Or at least it feels that way. But almost the universal response *du jour* is to lament and mourn the conflict. In fact, it seems that the only exception to this are a few WWF enthusiasts who never made it past fourth grade. Scan your Facebook feed for the past week, and count how many "sighs" and "groans" and "eye rolls" you can find, whether the post is directed at political conflict, theological conflict, or a believer's assertive mockery of some pagan aspect of modern culture. It's actually fairly rare to see measured but enthusiastic *engagement*. Often, we have the geez-guys-stop-your-culture-warmongering on the one hand, and on the other hand, mister-fire-brand-who-always-has-an-opinion-that-he-just-thought-up-five-seconds-ago-and-is-really-mad-that-nobody-else-understands-just-how-right-he-is. But there is another way.

The book of James is one place that paints a more complex picture for us. "From whence come wars and fightings among you? Come they not hence, even of your lusts that war in your members? Ye lust and have not: ye kill, and desire to have, and cannot obtain: ye fight and war, yet ye have not, because ye ask not" (Jas. 4:1–2).

James is familiar with the kind of people the descendants of Adam are: Not one of the sons of Adam falls far from the tree. There is more than a little bit of Cain in all of us. And James says that this kind of conflict comes from the fact that we are "adulterers and adulteresses." We are not faithful to our God, and our spiritual fornication is "enmity with God" (4:4). The reason we have fights with our brothers is because we are at war with the God who made us. How can we be at peace with one another if we are not at peace with God?

James is clear. There is a kind of conflict that flows directly out of our sinful natures, out of our lusts and unfaithfulness to God. Our response to this kind of conflict must be complete, heartfelt repentance: "God resisteth the proud, but giveth grace unto the humble. Submit yourselves therefore to God" (4:6–7). This is the kind of conflict that every Christian must mourn and lament (4:8–9). Those who swing their jealousies and lusts and greed around like a cat o' nine tails are murderers. Their tongues are a "world of iniquity . . . and it is set on fire of hell" (3:6).

The grace of God comes in the form of forgiveness. It comes in the form of being lifted up and set on solid ground. Whereas sinful conflict and striving is chaotic and uncertain, the peace of God is a fortress and a rock and all who seek refuge in Him cannot be moved. The grace of God also comes in the form of patience (Jas. 5:7). If lust and envy and greed are fundamentally various kinds of *impatience*, then repentance would be learning to wait on the Lord.

In the first century, Christians faced the enormous pressures of a Hellenistic pagan culture on the one hand and the growing extremes of the Jewish apostate culture on the other. As Paul's missionary journeys illustrate, Christians often found themselves on the losing end of tug-o-wars for power and influence in the cities of the empire. But the kinds of power and influence the Jews and Romans sought are not the weapons of our King. Patience is commitment to another way of life and a different kind of power.

This patience is not a pacifistic apathy. It's not stoicism or some kind of alternative Buddhism. This patience is grounded in the fact that "the coming of the Lord draweth nigh" and "the judge standeth before the door" (Jas. 5:8–9). Then James points to the prophets: "Take, my brethren, the prophets, who have spoken in the name of the Lord, for an example of suffering affliction, and of patience. Behold, we count them happy which endure . . . " (vv. 10–11).

Did you read that carefully? *Take the prophets for an example*. Which of the prophets lived a conflict-free life? Which of the prophets was not constantly in conflict with the enemies of God? Which of the prophets was known for his casual, mousy demeanor? Not one.

Take Elijah for an example, Christians, who when Ahab saw him said, "Are thou he that troubleth Israel?" (1 Kgs. 18:17). In fact, that title comes from the story of Achan who stole treasures from the plunder of Jericho. Joshua had commanded Israel not to take any of the plunder, specifically warning that anyone who did would bring "trouble" to Israel (Josh. 6:18). And because of this disobedience, Israel could not stand before their enemies, but turned their backs and fled before them (7:12). When Achan's sin was found out, Joshua asked, "Why hast thou troubled us? The Lord shall trouble thee this day" (7:25). And in that place where Achan and his family were executed, they raised up a great heap of stones and called the place "valley of Achor" which literally means "valley of trouble" (v. 26).

When Ahab calls Elijah the "troubler of Israel," he is accusing Elijah of being an Achan. In context, Elijah has proclaimed a severe drought in the land of Israel (1 Kgs. 17:1–7). The drought is so severe that only Elijah's prophetic authority spares the widow of Zarephath and her son (vv. 12ff). In other words, Ahab is not imagining troubles when he accuses Elijah. But Ahab dramatically misidentifies the source of the trouble. Elijah is clear: "I have not troubled Israel; but thou, and thy father's house, in that ye have forsaken the commandments of the Lord, and thou hast followed Baalim" (18:18). Elijah turns the tables and points his finger at Ahab. *You are the troubler of Israel. You are the Achan causing this disaster.*

Immediately following this episode, Elijah commands Ahab to assemble the four hundred and fifty prophets of Baal on Mount Carmel. And you know the rest of the story. But consider this: James has clearly, unmistakably preached against certain kinds of wars and fighting, the kind of conflict and striving that arises from the lusts and desires of the flesh. He has called the first century Christians to patience and endurance, and he points to the prophets. I'm afraid we read right over these verses and for some reason think that "prophets" means nice, Christian boy scouts who help old ladies across the street with their groceries.

Now don't get me wrong. I think Christians should care for the elderly, they most certainly must be gentle with the most vulnerable, binding up the broken hearts, comforting the afflicted. But James points to the *prophets*. The prophets married harlots. The prophets walked around Israel naked. The prophets proclaimed droughts. The prophets confronted politicians, religious leaders, and counseled defection to the enemies of Israel. The prophets foretold judgment and doom.

And just in case you're still looking for wiggle room in James, the last straw is the fact that the very next verse names a surprising prophet, a man named Job. Perhaps you haven't thought of Job as a prophet, but James certainly does. And given the end of the story, you should too. Clearly, part of the point is about straight-forward, patient endurance. Job endured much affliction before finally being vindicated by God in the final chapter of his story. But what I find so fascinating is that of all the prophets James might have highlighted, he chooses the one who spends thirtysome chapters *fighting* for his life with three Judas-like courtiers. What other book is full of such verbal wrangling? The book of Job is the original, divinely inspired blog war. And in the end, Job is rewarded for "speaking rightly," for blogging like the dickens, and refusing to back down or apologize (Job 42:7–15).

When a modern day Job speaks the truth and refuses to back down, the cries come up, *just apologize, admit you were wrong, and stop being such a culture-warrior.* The accusations are that this kind of faithful engagement only turns people off. *It's a bad witness. People don't like the Church because church people are mean and judgmental and angry.* But it's as though they cannot imagine a godly form of consternation. The only category they have is cranky or enraged, and I suspect this is because there's only an on/off switch in their own life. But if we are to follow the example of the prophets, then we must insist that when godly men and women get worked up, there is a way to do it in *a godly way*. This means they do not lose perspective, they do not lose sight of Jesus, they do not lose sight of the goals set before them. It's possible for a referee to enthusiastically call a foul without losing his temper and cussing a player out. It's possible to mock unbelief, pray for judgment, and share the gospel of Jesus Christ without losing days of sleep, without swearing under your breath, and without being grumpy with your wife or kids. It's not only possible—for Christians, it's absolutely necessary. This is the good fight of faith.

So God created man and armed him with a mouth. It's a flamethrower. It's a bazooka. But this is a design feature, not a factory defect. Of course sin complicates all of it, but part of the grace of salvation is Jesus' intention to redeem these weapons—to turn these cannons loose—on the demons of our day. In other words, if we were made to speak, we were made to fight.

That is what the gospel is *for*.

The concluding point: just as Jesus came to bring peace (but His peace disrupts), just as Jesus denounces the impulse to call fire down on cities in judgment (though His actions and words often brought severe upheaval), so too James, the brother of Jesus, urges the early Christians to repent of their lusts and wars, while emulating the prophets who proclaimed the judgments of God and resisted evil rulers with patience and joy. We must see both realities as aspects of faithfulness to the Word of God. This is the way of the real Jesus.

PART 2

THE IDOLS
THAT BLIND

CHAPTER 5

FEAR INCARNATE

Jesus and the apostles and prophets were men of courage. God sent them and us out into the world to open our mouths and make a holy ruckus for all evil and every kind of darkness. But this is not an easy, carefree existence, and there are temptations at every point to compromise, to ease up, to settle down. Nobody announces that they are going to compromise. It all begins very subtly. And the terrifying thing is that it frequently begins with a Bible verse used to defend it. The Devil prowls about as an angel of light. We begin reading the Bible selectively, which is to say, we begin to limit what we will let God say. We begin to limit

God's *authority*. It's much easier and more convenient to skim piously while underlining and highlighting the passages that make us feel happy and warm inside, or apply only to other people out there, because it's scary to do anything else. When we substitute faithfulness with this sort of cowardice, we do so telling ourselves that we're actually doing the right thing. In reality we have substituted the living God for an idol, but our idols are trimmed out in our pet theological frills. We call our compromise *boldness*, but it is actually fear. Idols are fear incarnate.

This lesson can be traced easily through the history of the children of Israel. Paul says that the history of Israel is a great cautionary tale: "Now these things were our examples, to the intent we should not lust after evil things, as they also lusted. Neither be ye idolaters, as were some of them . . . Now all these things happened unto them for ensamples: and they are written for our admonition, upon whom the ends of the world are come. Wherefore let him that thinketh he standeth take heed lest he fall" (1 Cor. 10:6–7, 11–12). Paul says that we should read the story of Israel and learn much, especially about idolatry. But we read the Old Testament and think they were a bunch of idiots for bowing down to statues and leaving fruit at totem poles over and over again. We think we stand because we are not tempted to pour out a libation in a pagan temple, and Paul says, take heed lest *you* fall.

So our first task in this section is to read what the Bible says about idolatry carefully. We want to ask God honestly whether we are tempted to worship idols, and if so, what would make them attractive, appealing, and seductive to *us*. How does the Devil approach modern Christians as an angel of light?

The Bible says that idols emerge from our fears. And in particular, they emerge from our failure to fear God and serve Him alone. Joshua commanded the people at the end of his life, "Now therefore fear the Lord, and serve him in sincerity and truth: and put away the gods which your fathers served on the other side of the flood, and in Egypt; and serve ye the Lord" (Josh. 24:14). But when the children of Israel followed other gods and served Baal and Ashtaroth, God "delivered them into the hands of spoilers that spoiled them, and he sold them into the hands of their enemies round about, so that they could not any longer stand before their enemies" (Judg. 2:14). When the Israelites came under bondage to the Midianites, God raised up a prophet who explained that their oppression was directly related to their fear of false gods: "And I said unto you, I am the Lord your God; fear not the gods of the Amorites, in whose land ye dwell: but ye have not obeyed my voice" (Judg. 6:6). When 2 Kings describes the people who remained in Samaria after Israel was carried away by the Assyrians, it condemns their compromised worship by appealing to the covenant with God:

> "With whom the Lord had made a covenant, and charged them, saying, Ye shall not fear other gods, nor bow yourselves to them, nor serve them, nor sacrifice to them: But the Lord, who brought you up out of the land of Egypt with great power and a stretched out arm, him shall ye fear, and him shall ye worship, and to him shall ye do sacrifice. And the statutes, and the ordinances, and the law, and the commandment, which he wrote for you, ye shall observe to do for evermore; and ye shall not fear other gods. And the covenant that I have made with you ye shall not forget; neither shall ye fear other gods." (2 Kgs. 17:35–38)

You shall not fear. You shall not *fear*.

The implication is clear: idolatry begins with fear. When people fear the other gods instead of the true God, they begin to bow down to them and serve them.

But why are people tempted to fear other gods? Because they are the gods of the people in power. They are the gods of the celebrities, the gods of the rich, the gods of the mighty, the gods of popular opinion.

What would happen if you didn't fear their gods? You would be passed up for promotions. You would be disinvited to their parties. You would be laughed at. You would be unfriended. And fear creeps in. If you say sodomy is sexual perversion in public, you might get fired. Are you afraid of losing your job? Are you afraid of not being able to get another job? Are you afraid of getting labeled? A fundamentalist? A right-wing extremist? Homophobic? What if you refuse to rent your apartment to a fornicating heterosexual couple? What if you get sued? What if you get fined for being a small-minded bigot? What if your business gets shut down? The pressure mounts pretty quickly to capitulate, to keep your head down, to shut up and keep your opinions to yourself. And let's face it: we're talking about livelihoods here. We're talking about your family, your children, your reputation in the community. And suddenly you wonder if you really are being a bigot. You begin to wonder what Jesus would do. He did warn against judging lest ye be judged, after all. And isn't God *unconditional* Love?

This is all to say that our problem is not fundamentally with our exegesis. Our problem is *illustrated* by our exegetical jukes, but our problem is much deeper than that. Jesus says it this way to the pastors and theologians of His day: "Ye have neither heard [the Father's] voice at any time, nor seen his shape. And ye have not his word abiding in you: for whom he hath sent, him ye believe not. Search the scriptures; for in them ye think ye have eternal life: and they are they which testify of me. And ye will not come to me, that ye might have life" (Jn. 6:37–39). Jesus says that the reason we don't hear God's word rightly is because we don't really believe in Him. We don't fear Him. But you can *pretend* to fear Him while reading the Bible. And then, when it starts getting uncomfortable, you can close the book. You can turn the page. You can do a Greek word study. But Jesus says that He is not a page that can be turned. Jesus is not a book that can be closed when it gets uncomfortable.

When Paul stood on Mars Hill in Athens, this was the conclusion of his sermon: God has appointed a day in which He will judge the world in righteousness by that man whom He has ordained, and the proof of this is the fact that God raised Him from the dead (Acts 17:31). God has appointed Jesus as judge of the world, and there is a day on which everyone will stand before Him. But notice that this is Paul's answer to all the idols in the city. "Now while Paul waited for them in Athens, his spirit was stirred in him, when he saw the city wholly given to idolatry" (v. 16). In other words, Paul's point about Jesus being the judge of every man is directly connected to the problem of idols. Paul explains, "Forasmuch then as we are the offspring of God, we ought not to think that the Godhead is like unto gold, or silver, or stone, graven by art and man's device. And the times of this ignorance God winked at; but now commandeth all men every where to repent . . . " (vv. 29–30).

What are gold and silver and art? They are memorials to the most valuable things, the most powerful things men have discovered and devised. Think of technology. Think of the stock market. Think of reputations. Think Nobel Peace prizes. Think of sex appeal. Think of political respectability. Think inner circles, elite, prestige. These are what idols are made of. And these are what people fear. We fear being rejected. We fear being scorned. We fear financial ruin. We fear loss of friends, family, security, happiness. Idols are hooks that get into the hearts of men long before they even open the Bible. Idols explain why religious people can be genuinely confused when Jesus shows up at their Bible study. *Sorry, who are you exactly?*

The fear of God, the fear of the real, living Jesus is the answer to our idol problem. Paul says that on the cross Jesus made a spectacle of all the principalities and powers because He triumphed over them in it (Col. 2:15). *Therefore*, Paul says, *let no man judge you.* That's what fear is. It's the fear of judgment. "There is no fear in love; but perfect love casteth out fear: because fear hath torment. He that feareth is not perfect in love" (1 Jn. 4:18). We fear the torments, the judgments of the gods, when we soften what the Bible actually says, when we side-step the hard questions, when we don't speak up for the truth. And we do it all in the name of love, in the name of having a good witness, in the name of seeking the peace of the city. Welcome to the problem. We are the problem.

It's easier to serve the gods of the nations. It's easier to make peace with the idols. And we pat ourselves on the backs and go to church on Sunday while leaving our offerings on the high places of human opinion and our pinches of incense at the groves of economic common sense. And we have the audacity to read about the Old Testament saints and shake our heads in disbelief that they couldn't shake themselves free of all that superstition. Yeah, unbelievable. It's hard to imagine people living their lives in fear of what others might think of them.

But ultimately, if we're really honest with ourselves, we prefer idols to Jesus because idols do not demand that we change. God commands all men everywhere to repent through His living Son Jesus Christ, but idols give us superficial assignments and leave us unchanged and lifeless.

CHAPTER 6

AUTONOMOUS ANTS

The first and most fundamental idol is named *self*. Self gets the award for most insidious, because it goes all the way down. It's wrapped into our identity, individuality, and consciousness as human beings. The first person is inescapable. Self-care and self-love are assumed, and even after we have relinquished all sovereignty over our own lives, the old idol Self can still show up unexpectedly, casually donning the uniform of piety, religion, sacrifice, even love.

However, every vestige of autonomy—submission to the authority of self—is simultaneously a *refusal to submit* to the exhaustive authority of Jesus. If we have lost the ability to speak with the authority of Jesus it is because we do not submit to the Jesus we keep talking about. But He is the Author of this story, the Designer and Inventor of this place. He is the Man in charge. He has given life to all men. And He is the Man that every last human being must finally come face to face with. He is the Man whom God has appointed to judge the world. There are no exceptions, there are no alternatives, there are no escape routes.

The first vestige of autonomy that must be sabotaged is any pride in your birthday. Oh sure, bake a cake, sing the song, and blow out your candles with a room full of family and friends and a glad heart. But "know ye that the Lord he is God: it is he that hath made us, and not we ourselves; we are his people, and the sheep of his pasture" (Ps. 100:3). Seems unnecessary to say, but the psalmist sings: *You didn't make yourself: God did.* Now you sing it.

Or another famous instance:

> For you formed my inward parts;
>> you knitted me together in my mother's womb.
> I praise you, for I am fearfully and wonderfully
>> made.
> Wonderful are your works;
>> my soul knows it very well.

My frame was not hidden from you,
when I was being made in secret,
   intricately woven in the depths of the earth.
Your eyes saw my unformed substance;
in your book were written, every one of them,
   the days that were formed for me,
    when as yet there was none of them.
   (Ps. 139:13–16, ESV)

And the psalm concludes with a prayer against the self: "Search me, O God, and know my heart: try me, and know my thoughts: And see if there be any grievous way in me, and lead me in the way everlasting" (vv. 23–24, ESV).

David knows that the first and primary enemy to "the way everlasting" is *inside of him*. Like David, we can't see Jesus clearly or hear Him accurately in the Scriptures because *we* get in the way. But one of the first shots God takes at our autonomy is the insistence that He made us, and that He has formed every single one of our days much like He knit us together in our mother's womb. God has written every one of our days, before there was a single one. As Job says, "Man that is born of a woman . . . his days are determined, the number of his months are with thee, thou has appointed his bounds that he cannot pass" (Job 14:1, 5).

In the modern world, evolution is the holy shrine of human autonomy. If this world accidentally fell out of the sky like a magical cow pie, and you happen to be a rational creature, it is up to you to determine the meaning of your life, your world, your existence. Here is the heart of autonomy: *Determine your own destiny, choose your own path, make your own meaning*. Of course in the first instance, this is like saying that since there is no such thing as language, you must create your own language. This is like saying that since beauty is pointless, you must invent your own beauty. Which is, how shall we put it . . . insane? But secondly, the implication is clearly a parody of the psalm: *Since God has not made us, we must make ourselves*.

Other books take up the biblical and scientific cases that can and should be made for the doctrine of creation. For now, we should merely note that reading evolution into the text of Genesis is a fabulous example of autonomy creeping into the Church. It may not appear as an overt attack on Scripture or God or Jesus, as it arrives in the garb of sophisticated interpretation, Hebrew studies, or scientific "me-too-ism." In Paul's day the center of these attacks came in the form of Judaizers, well-meaning believers who added traditional Jewish rituals and badges to the gospel of Christ

AUTONOMOUS ANTS | 67

alone: "Which things indeed have a show of wisdom in will-worship, and humility, and neglecting of the body, but they are of no value in stopping the indulgence of the flesh" (Col. 2:23, ESV). Similarly, Paul warns Timothy of perilous times when "men shall be lovers of their own selves . . . having a form of godliness, but denying the power thereof" (2 Tim. 3:2, 5).

Notice that the real issue is the relationship between worship and power, love and effectiveness. Autonomy is always a (false) offer of power and authority in exchange for some form of idolatry. In both of these passages, the worship and service is to the "self"—it is named "will-worship" in one and "lovers of self" in the other, but it amounts to the same thing: the self, the ego, retains ultimate jurisdiction. Bible verses are quoted, pious phrases repeated, but Self is still on the throne. Such men and women have an appearance of godliness, a show of wisdom, but both are ineffective and powerless in the end. They have a certain rhetorical power, but they lack the true power of the Spirit: "For God hath not given us the spirit of fear; but of power, and of love, and of a sound mind" (2 Tim. 1:7). If the Church is power*less* to proclaim the gospel and build the kingdom it is because we are lovers of self. We still cower and scrape at the god-self, the idol Self.

But God gives a power that is not fearful and is full of love and meaning. Paul encourages Timothy with these words: "Therefore do not be ashamed of the testimony about our Lord, nor of me his prisoner, but share in suffering for the gospel by the power of God, who saved us and called us to a holy calling, not because of our works but because of his own purpose and grace" (2 Tim. 1:8–9). Paul knows that even Timothy would be tempted to be ashamed of the gospel and the sufferings that attend it, but the power of God for resisting that shame flows out of a deep recognition of God's grace. Ironically, the shame actually flows out of a focus on our own works, but the power of God flows out of focusing on God's works. In other words, the real antidote to this will-worship and autonomy, the way God destroys the idol of self, is through the stunning reality of His goodness.

There you are, still breathing with lungs you didn't design, in an atmosphere perfectly balanced to keep you alive. These gifts are not random. These gifts are personal presents. They were wrapped with care and your name was written on the little tag. And not only did Jesus make you, He made all things (Col. 1:16). He fills all things, knows all things, and sees all things (Eph. 4:10). Jesus holds all things together and keeps them from flying apart (Heb. 1:3). It is God's sovereignty that demolishes every false human claim to autonomy.

"Or despisest thou the riches of his goodness and forbearance and longsuffering; not knowing that the goodness of God leadeth thee to repentance?" (Rom. 2:4). He gives you a glass of whole milk with a peanut butter and jelly sandwich. He gives you the sun falling through the window on a Saturday afternoon holding a million dancing dust particles. He gave you your wife and the way she smiles when you kiss her on the neck. He gave you your daughter and the way she giggles when you tickle her. Jesus gave you your son and the way he beams when you praise him. Jesus invented the hilarious way a child is conceived, and the mind-altering way babies are born. Jesus gives you deep joy and that gut-aching laughter that hurts so good. It's Jesus who shed His blood for the forgiveness of all your sins, and it's Jesus who crushes your whole being with the astonishing beauty of His mercy.

It is at the center of this goodness that Jesus says, "Do not be afraid." *Fear not, for I am with you.* But *we*—we suddenly look down and see the sheer impossibility of walking on water in the middle of a storm, and in our fear of the idols we lurch from the improbable to the absurd.

And absurdity is the other folly of autonomy. It is certainly unlikely that this world could come into existence. It's unlikely that *we* would come into existence. It's unlikely that we would function at all. It's unlikely that we would experience beauty and joy and taste goodness in our mouths. It's all impossible. But if there is a Maker, if there is One who means all of this, then as unlikely as it is, it is not incoherent. However, to suddenly insist that *now*, in this frightening moment, everything will fall apart if *we* do not seize the reins— *that* is absurd. Imagine the tiny ant that suddenly gets it into his nearly blind head that he must make the world mean something really important *right now*. And that is what autonomy is. That is what will-worship is. It has an appearance of wisdom and power, but it is actually an insane impossibility. How will the ant make sense of the universe? How will you wrap your head around it all? You can't and you won't, but the god Self wants to be appeased with food and sex and money and clothing and sleep and respect. And for one fading moment, it can feel like everything is awesome— until the buzz wears off and you're still just you and there's an empty feeling in your gut.

But Jesus confronts us. He confronts our idols with His reality, with His goodness, with His sharp grace.

He made us, and He has been raised from the dead and now sits at God's right hand. He has been appointed Judge of the whole earth. God commands all men everywhere to turn to Him. And if we come to Him, He will give us true life and power and wisdom.

CHAPTER 7

FIG LEAVES FOR JESUS

Idols are pious attempts to hide from Jesus.

You don't have to teach a two year old to say "mine!"—because no matter how cute they are, they still have sin in their bones. And we might get bigger and more sophisticated with our selfishness and sin, and our idols may get more expensive and fancy, but unless Jesus changes us, we're all selfish toddlers, demanding our own ways, demanding to be served, demanding sleep, demanding sex, demanding health and luxury and security and respect. These demands are still ultimately tied to autonomy—living by our own light, serving ourselves—but our games do get more elaborate.

When Adam and Eve sinned, they immediately hid from God because they were ashamed (Gen. 3:7). Of course when God called, they cleared their throats nervously, spread embarrassed smiles across their faces, and pretended everything was fine, casually pointing out that they had forgotten to put their skivvies on that morning—*but look, we found these nifty leaves*, they explained.

Some sons of Adam rage and kick against Him and fling their temper tantrums and curses to heaven for all the world to see and hear. They write angry books and letters, they perform kamikaze acts of terrorism, they lie, steal, and cheat with abandon. That's one way to do it. But it's a little obnoxious, not sustainable long-term, and generally not very attractive. And so the human race, being far more self-conscious and generally more sophisticated, tends to go the hypocritical route. Even Christians, those who profess faith in Jesus, who have tasted His potent grace, whose eyes have been opened to His goodness, are still tempted to try to keep Him at arm's length at times. The much more respectable way to keep Jesus off your case and to keep His grace out of your face is to go to church and go through the motions (or at least keep up some vague, warmed-over religious pretensions . . . maybe join the Boy Scouts or the Republican Party). In other words, religious people have a bad habit of hiding from Jesus in piles of religious trappings, with God-words, and whatever the Jesus-halo happens to be in their church ghetto: tucking their shirts in, fat theology books, homeschooling, ancient liturgies, Christian rock bands, Hebrew tattoos, organic farming, whatever. But when this happens, we begin serving idols.

Fig leaves are crutches, covers, Band-Aids for our souls, and they get in the way of the courageous witness we are called to have. Instead of standing boldly, telling the truth cheerfully, being persecuted and lied about and misunderstood, we take precautionary measures (with a Bible verse slapped on each one). We try to blunt the impact. We pat ourselves on the back and avoid the clash, avoid the conflict, avoid the point at which we would be left naked with only Christ our Righteousness as our royal robes. In other words, ironically, we avoid the very spotlight that would actually *be* our power and glory. We are afraid of not measuring up, afraid of being thought foolish, afraid of being misunderstood, and afraid of failure. So we strap on our buzzwords, our cultural uniforms, our security blankets, our idols, and we pretend everything is fine. But you can tell you're playing a game by the inconsistencies, by the hypocrisy, by the lack of gospel authority.

Maybe you're a pastor or a deacon in your church. Maybe you lead a community group. Maybe you got a golden star on your Sunday School chart or play guitar in the worship band. But do you yell at your wife? Do you dismiss her concerns as silly and foolish? Do you speak harshly to your children, criticizing and mocking them? Are you distant and cold toward your husband? Do you resent his hard work? Do you resent being home with the kids all day? Are you disrespectful to your parents? Do you roll your eyes at them and avoid talking? Do you tell your wife that your porn problem is not really a big deal? Do you drink too much and call it Christian liberty? Is your mouth full of filthy words and do you justify yourself because there isn't a list of bad words in the Bible? Are you a liar? Are you constantly spinning stories and covering things up and making yourself look better than you actually are? Are you a cheater? Do you steal from your employer? Are you bitter about the way your dad treated you, spoke to you, ignored you? Are you deeply envious of other people's success? Are you jealous of their jobs, their houses, their spouse, their children, their honor? You can't hide from Jesus. He knows everything and sees everything. He knows what you're really like. Your entire life is open and naked before Him.

Sin makes everything go wobbly. Nothing stays still. Nothing holds down. Everything begins to fall apart when you're hiding sin and resisting Jesus. And this is because you're not walking in the light. You're trying to maneuver in the dark. Or to change the image: Jesus said that people who don't listen to His word are like the man who tries to build his house on the sand (Mt. 7:26). The storms come and the house collapses. This was true of Israel as a whole, and it is still true of nations, churches, families, and individuals. When sin isn't dealt with, when it's allowed to fester and grow, disaster awaits you like a mugger in a dark alley. All have failed in some way or another. All are weak. All have let others down. All have hurt and been hurt. If anyone had the God's-eye movie of their life played on a big screen with all their thoughts and actions for all the world to see, every one of us would be absolutely horrified and embarrassed. We'd all be ashamed. So we put on makeup, we excel at business, we pick up hobbies, we get fancy cars or clothes, and we try to make up for our insecurity. We try to cover our shame, our nakedness. *I may have failed, but at least I'm in shape.*

I may have sinned, but at least I have money in the bank. I may have cheated, but at least I'm Reformed or have personal devotions or tithe or understand the sacraments or don't go to that other, stupid church. But those are all fig leaves. Economies crash, bodies fail, accomplishments fade, and you can't make up for your sin. It might be a real nice house, but you're building it on the sand.

Despite the fact that people try to hide, Jesus is still the great grace giver. "Moreover the law entered, that the offence might abound. But where sin abounded, grace did much more abound" (Rom. 5:20). God gave in the beginning in creation, jam-packing a universe full of presents and treasures and pleasures. And after we rejected Him, even in judgment there was mercy. His grace followed us into exile, and continued to pile up around us. Perfect, absolute justice would have been to just nuke the whole project. But instead, Jesus continued to speak the whole universe while giving people just enough space to feel the pain and agony and confusion of sin and death. But even then, it was always muted, restrained, meant to call us back to Him. *Where sin abounded, grace abounds more.*

So He kept giving, and eventually He came, born of a woman, crucified for sinners, to finally heal this broken, rotting world. So why are we pushing Him away?

Why are we avoiding Him? Because it hurts to have Him push where it's tender, where we're bruised or scarred, where we've sinned. We suspect He wants to perform surgery, and we avoid the appointment. We feign ignorance. We smile and point at how well we're doing everywhere else. We clear our throats nervously and point to the new line of fig-leaf skinny jeans, or the liturgy, or the praise band, or the evangelistic program. We want to be respectable, we want to do it ourselves, we don't want to fail, we want people to like us, we're afraid of being embarrassed, afraid of looking foolish, afraid of the sacrifice, afraid of the pain. But the irony is that we're hiding from *grace*. We're hiding from glory. We're avoiding the path to the cross, the path of Christian authority and power.

Besides, you cannot hide from Jesus. He sees through your fig leaves. You cannot hide from His grace, His Word, His blade. You may try to hide, to flinch, to push it away, to let it glance off you casually. But Jesus is alive. And you will meet Him. You will stand before Him. And His glory will smack you in the face and knock you down. His goodness is heavy. His grace is a sledgehammer. He will not leave you the same. But Jesus is a good man, the only good man, and you might as well come along cheerfully.

CHAPTER 8

WORSE THAN YOU THINK

Why do we try to cover our sin with fig leaves? Because we don't believe in God's grace. We're afraid His grace isn't actually sufficient for us, and we're afraid that His grace won't be sufficient for the world. We won't admit how bad we really are because then we won't be a good witness before the unbelieving world.

It's certainly true that Jesus said His followers are the light of the world and the Church is the salt of the earth (Mt. 5:13–14). But it's actually deeply ironic when we don't lead with the grace of forgiveness. Jesus says, *As the Church goes, so goes the world*. And we try to ignore sin and wonder why the world is full of darkness. We refuse to preach the grace of repentance from sin, and we wonder why the world loves sexual confusion, lies, and self-serving strife. We're teaching them how to disregard Scripture. We're teaching them that it's okay to nod our intellectual assent at pious platitudes while nursing our pet sins in secret. But regardless, Jesus still says that this world is our responsibility. We are responsible to provide the light. We are responsible to provide the flavor. We are the witnesses of a better way, the way of grace, the way of life.

But in order to repent of our blame shifting and abdication, we need to recognize how deep our complicity goes. And that is well illustrated by the simple fact that Jesus was murdered by church people. Not only that, there is a certain kind of spirituality and religiosity that is always a set up for this kind of bureaucratic evil.

If Jesus had been born in our day, the council that condemned Him as a blasphemous rabble-rouser would have included a couple of well-known evangelical pastors—one of whom was really into ancient liturgies—a few outspoken pro-life leaders, a conservative-libertarian-leaning politician, and at least one Bible-thumping fundamentalist. This is not because these convictions are inherently evil, but rather because self-righteousness *always* is.

Jesus was killed by the very people who claimed to serve Him. In fact, they killed Him believing that they *were* serving Him. He came to His own, but His own did not receive Him (Jn. 1:11). In other words, just because you go to church, have an awesome testimony, cried once during a killer worship song, got baptized by a well-known pastor, memorized the catechism, or follow St. Chrysostom's liturgy in the original Greek, doesn't mean all is well. If Jesus showed up today, there's no guarantee the Church wouldn't lead the crusade to have Jesus crucified again. And if you think that's ridiculous, chances are really good that things are actually much worse than you think.

The people of Israel were the people of God, the descendants of Abraham, the people of the promise, and when *their* God showed up in the flesh, they hated him and killed him. Talk about friendly fire . . . only it wasn't an accident.

Jesus made this point in a parable about the chief priests and Pharisees: They were the vineyard workers. They ran all the Israelite discipleship programs and published the Bible study guides. They were the pastors, the community group leaders, the worship leaders, the choir directors, the youth ministers, the conference speakers, but when God, the owner of the vineyard, sent servants to collect the fruit, they were beaten and rejected. Finally, when the owner sent His own Son in hopes that they would at least respect Him, the vineyard workers killed the heir, hoping that would put an end to the annoying visits (Mt. 21:34–41).

Let's trace this carefully. People don't wake up one morning and decide to murder the Son of God. There were many small compromises along the way, and the common denominator in all of them is the failure to deal with sin the way God says to. In the flesh, people want to cover their sin with some kind of good works, with something spiritual or holy. This is self-righteousness. It may be traditional liturgy, trendy praise choruses, preachers in suits, preachers in robes, preachers in skinny jeans and black-rimmed glasses. It might be traditional, it might be contemporary, it might be trendy, it might be scholarly, it might be slick, it might be sloppy. But whatever Jesus used last, whatever the Spirit seemed to fill most recently, people latch on to the form, the carrier, the vessel, the dress code, the method, and they try to manufacture power by their own righteousness.

This is what Isaiah was talking about:

> To what purpose is the multitude of your sacrifices unto me? Saith the Lord: I am full of the burnt offerings of rams, and the fat of fed beasts; and I delight not in the blood of bullocks, or of lambs, or of he goats. When ye come to appear before me, who hath required this at your hand, to tread my courts? Bring no more vain oblations; incense is an abomination unto me; the new moons and sabbaths, the calling of assemblies, I cannot away with; it is iniquity, even the solemn meeting. Your new moons and your appointed feasts my soul hateth: they are a trouble unto me; I am weary to bear them. And when ye spread forth your hands, I will hid mine eyes from you: yea, when ye make many prayers, I will not hear: your hands are full of blood." (Is. 1:11–15)

There is a tendency deep in the souls of the descendants of Adam that wants nothing to do with God Himself, because then they would have to actually trust Him. They would have to let go of their fears and trust His grace. They would have to admit their complete helplessness and thorough sinfulness. So people try to bottle Him, to leash Him. We don't want to trust Him; we want to trust *ourselves* while we continue talking a lot about trusting Him, worshiping Him, praying to Him. This insecurity has a death grip on people, and we cling to this feeling of control and come to hate whatever might loosen that hold. The challenging thing is that whatever we're holding on to is often quite harmless in itself, even a positive good. Who commanded the Israelites to offer all those sacrifices and incense? *God did.* But He commanded that worship to be offered sincerely, with humility, with true faith, clinging to Him. Like Isaiah, Jesus said the same thing about the scribes and Pharisees: they are whitewashed tombs that really are quite impressive to look at (Mt. 23:27). But turns out that self-righteousness is the kind of sin that follows the dress code and has chameleon manners and is the favorite cover for a rotting corpse. And God hates it.

Jesus totally wrecked the name "Pharisee," and now nobody wants that title, but before Jesus showed up, it would have been somewhat synonymous with "evangelical" and "seminary professor" and "Reformed" and "church person." But when Jesus came in with His jackhammer and wrecking ball, He set them up outside their schools and churches and said *they* were the problem with the world. They were infested with demons. When they gathered for worship, the temple became a den of thieves, fresh in from the latest hit job.

How is this possible?

Jesus says that the Jews rejected Him because although they knew a lot about God, they didn't actually *know* God. God wasn't actually their Father, even though they claimed otherwise. They were bastards (Jn. 8:38–42). Jesus said that their dad was actually the Devil, and that's why they wanted to kill Him. Children know their fathers' voices, they speak their language, and the rhythms and tonality comfort them. But when Jesus—the only begotten Word of the Father—came, the Jews could not stand it. His voice was an offensive noise, and as with Stephen, they plugged their ears and ran together at Him, cast Him out of the city, and put Him to death just to get Him to stop talking (cf. Acts. 7:57).

This is why Paul writes to Timothy and warns him that in the Church there will be men who are lovers of themselves, lovers of money, boasters, proud, unloving, unforgiving, brutal, traitors, headstrong and haughty, and Paul says—and this is crucial—that these men will have a "form of godliness." They will have learned the catechism questions and passed seminary classes and become members of the church and homeschooled their children and been pro-life. But this form of godliness will not be the real thing, because they will deny its power. And Paul says to stay far away from those people. But they will put on such a good show that they will creep into households and make captives of gullible women, loaded down with sins (2 Tim. 3:1–7).

In other words, we need to be a lot more suspicious of ourselves. It's not enough to go to church, get baptized, or run a Christian school. You aren't safe because your parents were Christians, because you say "gospel-centered" a lot, and can find Jesus typology in Quentin Tarantino films, and can lead a small group Bible study. We must insist on real gospel *power*, and that power comes straight from God's grace dealing with our sin.

This realization—that people are worse than they generally think—doesn't create mousy, tentative, pencil-necked men. On the contrary, the Apostle Paul insists that it was the depth of his own previous sin and rebellion that made room for all the grace. When people give their testimonies in the modern Church, they get teary-eyed and think they aren't worthy to ask the youth pastor about his enthusiastic hugs with the high-school girls. But when Paul gives his testimony, it charges him up and he gets rowdy with righteousness. "This is a faithful saying, and worthy of all acceptation, that Christ Jesus came into the world to save sinners; of whom I am chief. Howbeit for this cause I obtained mercy, that in me first Jesus Christ might shew forth all longsuffering, for a pattern to them which should hereafter believe on him to everlasting life" (1 Tim. 1:15–16). Notice that Paul maximizes his own sin—*it's worse than you think*—in order to make room for us. If Jesus can save a sinner like Paul, then He can save sinners like us.

But that's not all. The kind of mercy that Jesus shows is a full-rehabilitation mercy. The fact that Paul was formerly a blasphemer, a persecutor, an insolent opponent, is not opposed to the very next command he gives: "This charge I commit unto thee, son Timothy . . . that thou mightest war a good warfare; holding faith, and a good conscience; which some having put away concerning faith have made shipwreck" (1 Tim. 1:18–19). Paul magnifies God's grace by magnifying his own sin. And that *grace* is the basis for the authority on which Paul stands to charge Timothy to go to war with all sin and unbelief.

There's a demonic tendency in the descendants of Adam to want to paper over our sin because we don't really believe in the grace of God. We act like God's grace is for extreme circumstances and we spend our days trying to gin up our own grace, our own forms of godliness, to *prove* our righteousness. And we wonder why we're so weak and powerless. But Paul says, "I am the least of the apostles, that am not meet to be called an apostle because I persecuted the church of God, but by the grace of God I am what I am: and his grace which was bestowed upon me was not in vain; but I labored more abundantly than they all: yet not I, but the grace of God which was with me" (1 Cor. 15:9–10). Paul worked harder and got more done than all the other apostles because God's grace was great toward him. The worse the sin, the greater the grace, and the greater the grace, the more potent the power.

Or, as Jesus says, those who have been forgiven much love much. Christian love is not a Hallmark card. Christian love is a bloody cross for undeserving sinners. This is the source of true Christian power. When God blesses His people, there will always be form: there will always be liturgy and tradition and customs. But everything hinges on what you think makes you great, what you think makes you powerful.

Jesus says His cross makes us strong; His blood makes us bold. It's not your programs. It's not your politics. It's not your goodness. It's all His grace. That's what turns the darkness of the world into light. That's the sort of salt the world needs.

CHAPTER 9

PREACHING PEOPLE INTO THE GRAVE

We don't like being as bad as the gospel actually says we are. So we prop up our egos with various kinds of idols that are (pseudo-) piously calculated to blunt the extreme grace of God. But then we are no good at preaching the real gospel to anyone else. If we refuse to let the grace of Jesus stab all the way through our hearts, why would we be any good at driving the same sword into those around us? You end up with one of two errors. The first is high-handed hypocrisy, requiring burdens of others that you would not lift with your little finger—this frequently comes out in highly legalistic and harsh church cultures. But the other error seems to plague most of our churches, and that is piles of churches with a bland, superficial grace that isn't sharp enough to cut anything. All of this serves to underline the fact that many Christians are trying to follow Jesus without actually dying—but the message of the gospel is that they're already dead.

Pagan courage feared the grave and made its uneasy peace with the inevitability of Hades, but Christian courage is born in the grave. Christian courage begins with the reality of death. The central offense of our Good News is that people apart from the grace of God are dead. Not a little bit dead, not slightly dead, not mostly dead. *Dead* dead. Everybody descended from Adam—every last man, women, and child—is dead. Our dead hearts are swarming with the foul maggots of lust and lies and bitterness (Eph. 2:1). Apart from Jesus commanding us to rise up and walk, we are corpses, rotting dutifully in our graves, and all we have to offer is the stench of death.

When we don't preach and teach the full offense of this gospel tearing the pride of man all the way down to the ground, what we are actually doing is leaving him unprotected. We are leaving his most insidious idolatry fully functioning. In the name of being nice, in the name of being polite, in the name of not offending, we leave his pride intact, which is his Achilles' heel. It is the very thing that must die in order for him to truly live. And this is because Jesus only calls the dead to life. He raises the *dead* by the powerful working of the Holy Spirit.

In the trenches of life, we can't see peoples' hearts. We can't always tell where they're at. But our job is to believe the gospel and preach the grace of Jesus. We must not dilute it. We must not downplay it. We must not settle for a dim and dusty basement when the gospel is actually nothing but pure, blinding light. We must not settle for pop-its when the Spirit is a nuclear explosion. We may not make excuses or explain away our failures with phrases like "besetting sins" and "weakness." The gospel is that every human heart is a rock-hard, barren land completely unreceptive to the word of God, and we are told that it is the preaching of the gospel, the proclamation of the love of God in Jesus that softens hearts and raises the dead.

Ezekiel was told to preach to dry bones (Ezek. 37). Paul says we were dead in our trespasses and sins (Col. 2:13). Isaiah was told to preach until all of Israel was one big handicap convention (Is. 6:9–10), and Jesus takes up that same mantle in the gospels (Mk. 4:12).

While there are immediate historical aims, which may include temporal judgment (bad guys destroying Jerusalem), the ultimate end is the salvation of Israel. The ultimate end is to raise the dead, give sight to the blind, open the ears of the deaf, and unloose the tongue of the dumb (Lk. 4:18–19). But this means, putting all of this together, that the intermediate step in getting there (salvation) is preaching people into their graves: preaching their eyes blind, their ears deaf, their tongues completely tied, their pride dead. This means preaching the utter futility of all your programs, all your mission statements, all your evangelism, all your sacraments, all your liturgies, all your worship bands, all your seminary classes, all your natural good looks, all your personality gifts, and all your contextualized crap.

The gospel is the efficacious announcement of *death first*. It's the proclamation that everyone is worse than they think, and all our coolest stuff is filthy rags compared to His glory. And Jesus says that this announcement actually performs what it announces. It is an authoritative announcement like "I now pronounce you man and wife." The evangelist always begins with the authoritative announcement "You are dead." And sometimes the dead people do nothing because, well, they are dead. Sometimes they convulse a bit like some kind of frankenmummy before going back into rot mode. And sometimes they sit up and suck in mouthfuls of clean, fresh air and begin to live. And sometimes this happens in the middle of a traditional hymn, sometimes it happens in the middle of a sermon, sometimes it happens at a baptism, sometimes it happens in the car on the way home from committing adultery.

This is what Christian baptism means. Paul says that the Romans were baptized into the death and resurrection of Jesus Christ (Rom. 6:3–4). In the first instance, it proclaims death. We preach and counsel people into the grave. And their greatest problem is that they don't believe it. They don't believe they are dead. They don't believe they are rotting corpses. They don't believe they are as bad as that. But the crucifixion of Jesus means they are actually worse than they think. And this brings us back to our refrain: this is hardest for people inside the church, who live in respectable, middle class suburbia, who know their catechisms and have memorized the liturgy, who know the buzzwords, and when to raise their hands during the song with the really sweet chord progression. But there's a demonic Amalekite Pharisee in every human heart that needs to have Jesus come like a righteous Samuel and hack that punk to pieces.

We are not here to put on a show. We are not here to look respectable. We are not here to punch our religious cards. We are here because a man named Jesus has taken away our sins, and now we are blameless. We were blind, but now we see. We were lost, but now we are found. We are here because Jesus is God in the flesh, and He was crucified for us and on the third day rose up from the dead. We are here because of the love of God, and specifically, the power of that love that takes away our sin and makes the foulest clean.

Sometimes people are concerned that if we question our programs, our worship, our evangelism, our mercy ministry, the sacraments, won't that teach people to doubt? Won't it invite people to fear? But this is no ordinary grave we preach them into. This is no ordinary darkness we proclaim. We preach the darkness that fell over the world at the death of the crucified Lamb of God. We preach the grave of the only innocent man in the history of the world. We insist that this is what baptism means, but because we know our own hearts and because we know the deceitfulness of the flesh, we insist that it is not enough to merely have some kind of superficial ascent to this "theology." We *may not* go through the motions. We insist that our own foul stench fill our nostrils, our own rebellion kick us in the gut, because only when people see that they are actually dead can they begin to live, only when they come to grips with their rebellion can they understand forgiveness, only when they realize that they are not worthy to be called sons will they feel their Father's embrace. The only way to live is to die. The only way to find life is to lose it.

You must come to the end of yourself, come to the end of your goodness, come to the end so that you can finally begin. And for those who know Jesus, the grave of Jesus is no scary place. The grave of Jesus is glory and wonder, because the grave of Jesus is empty. And once you've died with Jesus, you aren't afraid of anyone or anything anymore.

CHAPTER 10

GRACE HAS A BEARD

Let's face it: we're all theological perfectionists. This is partly because we're lazy and it sounds pious to excuse ourselves by pointing out that we don't have the right tool. And it is partly because we've let cranky Euclidian engineers run our theology departments (nothing against cheerful Euclidian engineers, honest).

We think theology is the task of keeping everything organized into pristine categories rather than thinking of those categories as tools that may or may not apply to any number of concrete circumstances. The end result is that we often flip the problems on their heads and demand that situations conform to the tools we have come up with. And when anything might be construed as messy, sloppy, or misunderstood, we call the whole enterprise off—*we don't have the right tool*, we shrug. But the offense of the gospel, and the offense of Christian faithfulness, is the insistence that grace touches down in this world. It incarnates. It particularizes. It deals with particular people in real time. This was foolishness to the Greeks, and it's still foolishness to anyone with eyes in their heads.

As I write, the well-known young-earth creationist Ken Ham just debated Bill Nye ("The Science Guy") in a highly publicized showdown. Following the debate, all the critics weighed in. And as you may imagine, there likely weren't any dramatic conversions on the spot. But one noticeable result was that Christian cannibalism set in. It doesn't even matter what the particular objections were: the fact remains that a Bible-believing Christian stood up in front of the world and faithfully confessed Christ in the face of staggering unbelief . . . and piles of *Christians* started whining. But grace always shows up in particular people, in particular places, at particular times and in wonderfully imperfect ways. This doesn't mean we never offer correctives or input or suggestions, but there's a certain kind of tone deafness that can't tell the difference between David tuning his harp and John Cage recording his own heavy breathing. He who has ears to hear, let him hear.

People make all kinds of excuses. *The quality was not great. He sidestepped the real issues. I don't like his style.* Whatever. But the reason we won't have grace touch down, particularizing and incarnating, is because it's a threat. It's a threat to my autonomy. It's a threat to my reputation. It's a threat to the tiny kingdom here in my heart. All that Jesus stuff—that's out *there*, up in the sky, in tidy categories that probably mostly apply to other people somewhere (probably in federal penitentiaries), so it can't mess with me. And (related to what we just covered in the previous chapter), I can verbally assent to needing "Jesus" for that kind of sinfulness without actually letting Him knock my teeth out.

Years ago, Don Fairbairn taught me that the early Christians came to explain *who* Jesus is by *what* we needed Him to do. If Jesus is the Rescue Mission of God for this sorry, messed-up world, the precise tool we need to solve our human problem, then *Who* He is tells us a lot about what the problem is, and vice versa. We've already insisted that our problem is that we're dead. God doesn't meet us halfway with ideas and generalities and universal principles. God's solution is not an herbal remedy regimen or a rehab program. Nutritionists and oncologists and therapists don't spend much time in morgues, and no one calls 911 upon finding a cemetery filled with dead people. Just to be clear, that's because *it's already too late*. Nobody specializes in corpses except for morticians, and they don't do rehabilitation.

When we resent the particularity of the gospel in the messiness of real life, we make two big errors. First, we betray our preference for a rehab program where we study this information, we change our habits, and *voilà*, we're alive again, in which case, Jesus can just be your therapist, a teacher, a coach—he doesn't need to be a particular man at a particular place and time. You just need new information, more information, and a warm feeling in your belly. But particular people have committed particular sins. And every particular place where the curse of sin has touched down, God is determined to heal it and put it right—with a particular man. The real Jesus is not an idea, not a force, not a feeling. Jesus is not a theology program, a philosophy, a ritual, or a chord progression. Fundamentally, Jesus is God-as-a-man. Jesus is the infinite God with two eyes and two ears, ten fingers and ten toes. Jesus is the eternal God with a beard and a belly button. This is the real Jesus.

Second, by resenting the particularity of the gospel, we refuse the weapons of the Spirit. It's like we're playing baseball, but we refuse to swing the bat. We watch strike after strike whizzing by, but they're never good enough. We have imagined the perfect pitch and the perfect swing . . . but we refuse to swing. And we have ready rants for all the other players who swing away. *Rah, rah, you strike out a lot. You swing at bad pitches. Your stance is too open.* But the real reason we refuse to swing, the real reason we refuse to accept that God works through normal people taking their best cuts at the ball, is because that would reveal that *we* are just normal people. We'd end up swinging at bad pitches occasionally and striking out and hitting into double plays. It would make us look bad. Which just goes to show that our pride is not yet all the way dead. So kill it, bro.

The grace of God, His holy cheer and eternal delight and loving-kindness, *got born*. It was conceived in the womb of a teenage Jewish girl, who was engaged to be married to a respectable (if poor) Galilean carpenter. The Holy Spirit put that grace there to develop for nine months. And that woman, named Mary, gave birth to her Son and named Him Jesus, because He was born to save the world from their sins. "And the Word became flesh and dwelt among us, and we beheld His glory, the glory as of the only begotten of the Father, full of grace and truth" (Jn. 1:14). This is the *grace* of God. This is His smile. Grace is a man named Jesus.

So what does that mean in regard to idols?

First, it means that Jesus is Lord: the most basic Christian confession of faith (1 Cor. 12:3). He is not just *a* lord among many. He's not running for the position or lobbying for votes. He's not a hopeful. He is Lord of all (Acts 10:36). He is King, Master, Sovereign, Lord, over everything and everyone. No exceptions. After He had humbled himself to be born as a man, becoming an obedient servant, He died, humiliated and cursed, on the cross, and therefore, God His Father has highly exalted Him and given Him the name that is above every name (Phil. 2:5–7). And this exaltation includes the promise that every knee will bow and every tongue confess that He is Lord (Phil. 2:10–11). And the implication for the world, for us, is that we *need* a Lord. We don't want a Lord; we resent not being the lord ourselves. But Jesus is Lord for all the traitors, too. He's the Lord of economics and politics. He's the Lord of philosophy and history. He's the Lord of parenting and marriage. He's the Lord of Honduras, Sweden, Pakistan, Uganda, and everything in between. He's the Lord of your thoughts, your desires, your dreams, your pain. He is Lord, and you need Him to be Lord.

Second, we need to emphasize that the incarnation—the fact that God was born as a particular man named Jesus—is not at all at odds with this lordship. The fact that God became a slave and went obedient to His unjust execution is not opposed to His being God or being sovereign. It's not as though the incarnation was an intermission in the normal course of God being in charge. At no point during the story was Jesus less than God. He always had the right to demand to be honored as God. It would not have been robbery to claim to be equal with God. In fact, at several points, Jesus pretty much came out and said so, and the Jews got pretty ticked (Jn. 5:17–18, 8:56–59, 10:38–39). In fact, the incarnation is actually the very point at which we see God *as God*. It's the very point at which God shows His face to us directly *as Lord*. The Word of God that sung creation into being, the Word that thundered at Sinai, the Glory-Word that roared in the tabernacle and temple has become flesh and dwelt among us. *And we beheld His glory, the glory as of the only begotten of the Father.*

Third, if God Himself was *displayed* in coming down to us, in being born a baby, in suffering and dying and rising again at a particular place on the map, at a particular point in time, then He is not merely the Lord of Heaven—Lord of decrees and commands and unapproachable light. That same Lord of Heaven is also Lord of Earth. That same Lord of decrees and commands is the Lord of healing and blessing and bread-multiplying and table-tossing. The Lord of unapproachable light has even gone down into the unimaginable darkness. But it's not merely that He can do both, rather, the real glory is that He does one by means of the other. He is God *by* being born a baby. He is the Lord *by* humbling Himself to death. He is the Light *by* going down into the darkness. He is the humble servant *by* driving the merchants out of the temple. God's grace touches down, and if it doesn't touch down, it isn't grace.

A particular Jesus means these three things. And this is why you can raise your hand in class and question your professor's arrogant atheism. God shows up in those moments when we need Him. This is why you can share the gospel with your angry dad. Jesus is Lord there. This is why you can confess that dark, haunting sin. Jesus was there when it happened, and He will carry you all the way into the light. This is why you can invite your homosexual neighbors over for dinner. Grace touches down. This is why you can preach the gospel with authority and abandon. This is why you can mock cultural folly. If God has proclaimed His authority, His power, His lordship over all things by entering into the particularity of this world, then you can and must do the same.

Do you see that?

Do not wait for the perfect pitch. Do not resent the messiness of this life. If God stooped to be Lord of the universe from the womb of a virgin, then you can and must trust Him to be Lord in whatever circumstances you find yourself in. Listen to Paul's glorious testimony: "Last of all, as to one untimely born, he appeared also to me. For I am not worthy to be called an apostle, because I persecuted the church of God. But by the grace of God *I am what I am*, and his grace toward me was not in vain . . . " (1 Cor. 15:8–10). *You are who you are*. You were made. You were thought up by Jesus. He intends to be Lord in you, through you. His grace is not in vain. You will whiff embarrassingly. You will strike out. You will. But that's why Jesus came. You are free to fail, free to be faithful where you are, free to swing away. Who knows what your part is? But you can be sure nobody ever hit a home run without swinging.

CHAPTER 11

GOD-SHAPED BOLDNESS

If the general theme of the preceding chapters is a number of different angles on the idols of self and self-sufficiency and self-righteousness, we finish this section with the insistence that the lordship of Jesus makes believers bold. But this is no ordinary boldness, this is a boldness uniquely shaped by the way God is at work in the world.

The point is well illustrated by the baptizer of Jesus himself. The Son of God was baptized at the edge of a small, muddy river called Jordan by a grasshopper-eating prophet with a bad attitude and a hair shirt. Was John the Baptizer really the best front man for the Kingdom of God? This is God's idea of conquest. He pushes past all our yellow tape and orange cones. And He does it because He can, because He made this place, and because we've made peace with idols that He's intent on smashing.

There are at least two lessons we need to learn from this: First, we need to understand God's style of conquest—why He breaks certain rules and yet isn't guilty of anarchy. And second: if the Church will follow and love her Lord, we must embrace this way of doing business.

Now, this is not a defense of sloppiness. I am not making a case for running red lights or going off grid and forming neo-monastic militia communes in the wilderness of North Dakota. However, we *are* talking about some of the basic principles that would include righteous civil disobedience at points—the sorts of principles that could land you in jail, lose you your job, or get you slapped with a certain reputation that won't get you invitations to certain parties. As we have noted periodically, wisdom is something between all the errors, something that may be easily mistaken for the extremes. But what we must refuse to do is tame this Jesus. We must refuse to sand off the sharp edges. We must not sing songs that declare Him Lord and then nervously clear our throats when He raises up a hick family of bearded duck hunters to tell the truth about human sexuality.

Jesus was Lord growing up a faithful carpenter's son, and He was Lord when He gave His parents the slip in order to give the scribes and priests some Sunday School lessons during Passover. He cast demons into pigs and ruined a local economy, insulted respected theologians, walked across bodies of water, raised the dead in order to pick a fight, broke Sabbath rules, healed certain sick people to make other people mad, claimed that His flesh and blood were food and drink, comforted the mourning, paid no attention to purity laws when He didn't want to, fed thousands with some poor kid's sack lunch, and talked to storms about their rambunctious habits on the Sea of Galilee. Then, because He could, He laid His life down. The Lord of Life voluntarily released the reins of life, allowing death, Hell, sin, Satan, all the other principalities and powers to do their worst. No one in the history of the world would write this story. No one would come up with this. It is not safe. It is not tidy. It doesn't fit into anybody's systematic theology. People could get the wrong idea all the time. And all the people with prefab programs and systems and uniforms are the bad guys.

It was kind of cute, in a sad sort of way—watching the big, strong Jews and Romans all dressed up in their fancy getups with their formal paperwork and books of church order and committees and websites. Kind of like kindergartners on their first day of school, hair sticking up in the back, a bit of jelly smeared on their cheeks, with their tongues sticking out, forming their letters just so and getting a little huffy about it. They did their best, they did their worst, and they were wicked, cruel, and sick. And had they known what they were doing, they would have never done it (1 Cor. 2:8).

Then, because He could, He took His life back up again (Jn. 10:17). In fact, Jesus says that this is one of His Father's favorite things—"Therefore My Father loves Me." Jesus says that death and resurrection is one of His Father's favorite tricks. You almost get the idea that He might think it would be fun to do again. Jesus laid His life down because He was Lord, and He took it back up again because He is Lord. From conception to birth, from childhood to manhood, from storms to deformities, from fear to pride, from life to death (and back), Jesus claims it all. He has embraced it all, won it all, conquered it all, and therefore rightfully rules in and through it all.

And the theme is *impossibility*. The theme is breaking the rules, pushing the limits, leaping the chasms left by sin, death, and Satan. His grace is unstoppable. Death and resurrection is His favorite.

But the Bible also repeatedly gives us clues and hints as to what is going on behind the scenes of all God's "rule breaking." And that theme is *loyalty*. Jesus is not merely ditching his parents for a joy ride in Jerusalem. He gives His parents the slip because He needs to be about His Father's business (Lk. 2:49). Jesus says that everything He does is about His Father's will: "I can of mine own self do nothing: as I hear, I judge: and my judgment is just; because I seek not mine own will, but the will of the Father which hath sent me" (Jn. 5:30). And Jesus insists that His disciples do the same: "If any man come to me, and hate not his father, and mother, and wife, and children, and brethren, and sisters, yea, and his own life also, he cannot be my disciple" (Lk. 14:26). The point is that the disciples of Jesus must be as loyal to His Father as He is. And disloyalty is all about being loyal to a *different* father: "I speak that which I have seen with my Father: and ye do that which ye have seen with your father" (Jn. 8:38). The boldness of Jesus is rooted in His loyalty to His Father, and all truly Christian boldness is the same.

Absolute loyalty means insisting that Jesus is Lord. When the first disciples said that Jesus is Lord, they were insisting that Jesus—against all odds—is alive from the dead (Acts 2:32–36). Jesus says, "I am He who lives, and was dead, and behold I am alive forevermore. Amen. And I have the keys of Hades and of Death" (Rev. 1:17–18). This is how we know that God can be trusted: He raised Jesus from the dead. This is why when the chief priests demanded that they stop preaching this Jesus, the apostles smirked a little and said (roughly), "We ought to obey God rather than men, because God raised Jesus from the dead, the same Jesus you guys murdered" (Acts 5:29). In fact, Peter explains that the reason they won't be obeying the Jewish council on this matter is because God has exalted Jesus to his right hand and made him Prince and Savior for the forgiveness of sins (Acts 5:31). It is the lordship of Jesus that authorizes the apostles to disobey human authorities, and it is the forgiveness of Jesus that has inspired their loyalty. Shortly before this, when Peter and John were first arrested, they proclaimed this same message to the elders of Israel, announcing that there is no other name under heaven given among men, whereby we must be saved (Acts 4:12). This boldness, this fearlessness did not come upon Peter and John merely because they were apostles. No, Luke tells us explicitly that the elders of the Jews marveled when they realized they were "unlearned and ignorant men," but they knew that they spoke with such boldness because "they had been with Jesus" (Acts 4:13). This is boldness that comes from spending time with Jesus.

When the apostles were released, they gathered together for prayer and worship, and they understood that what happened to Jesus was exactly what David had foretold in Psalm 2: "The kings of the earth stood up, and the rulers were gathered together against the Lord and against his Christ. For of a truth against thy holy child Jesus, whom thou has anointed, both Herod and Pontius Pilate, with the Gentiles, and the people of Israel, were gathered together" (Acts 4:26–27). And they prayed for more boldness because it all happened according to the plan of God, and by that plan they expected Jesus to continue performing signs and wonders through them (vv. 28–30).

The story of the incarnation is the story of God's power and authority over all things. This power is not a blustering tyranny or a loud-mouthed despotism. This power is manifested in what looks like weakness and impossibility. And this is the blueprint of our salvation.

Jesus said, "Behold, I make all things new." All things includes divorce, rape, false accusations, genocide, suffering, disease, malnutrition, misunderstanding, honest mistakes, utter failure, vindictive backstabbing, adultery, lies, corruption, manipulation, all injustice, and everything in between. In other words, the brokenness extends to all things in this world, and Jesus is not surprised or inhibited by any of it. Jesus is undaunted. There is no shadow in any corner of the universe that the Light of Easter can be kept out of. God's loyalty, God's love comes hunting for it all. And precisely where we say *it cannot be done, it probably ought not to be done, it's not safe, are you allowed to do that?* His grace breaks through. His life breaks in.

So where is God calling you to be bold, to pray for big things, to work for impossible things? What sin is He asking you to address? Which idol is He insisting you tear down?

PART 3
THE MISSION

CHAPTER 12

NO PARACHUTES

S o we have sketched the outlines of our idolatry, and now we turn toward the project of proclaiming a positive vision of the Christian life. This is the broad and admittedly over-ambitious aim of the last half of this book. How do we begin to trust Jesus as we ought? How do we follow Him? How do we lean into this life and begin to imitate our Savior?

The first step is ditching our parachutes.

The Spirit of God is His breath. God is the Wind that hovers over the waters of the deep, the Wind that rushes over the world, creating, sustaining, renewing all things (Gen. 1:2). God rides on the wings of the wind (Ps. 18:10). He commands the stormy wind; He causes it to lift the waves of the sea (Ps. 104:3). Not only did a giant thunderhead lead Israel out of Egypt, when the Lord descended on Sinai, He came like a rambunctious storm (Exod. 19:16–19). A tornado killed Job's children, and then when the Lord finally answered Job, He called to him from the whirlwind (Job 38:1). When the Spirit descended at the first Pentecost, He came like an electrical storm, a hurricane of fire and rushing wind (Acts 2:2–3).

It's all hip and trendy to talk about having a personal relationship with Jesus, asking Him into your heart, getting saved, being born again. And of course, you must be born again, you must be saved, you must know Jesus and walk with Him (Jn. 14:6, 1 Jn. 5:20). There is no other life. There is no other way. But have you ever stopped to consider what that actually means?

Noah found grace in the eyes of the Lord and was commissioned to build an enormous floating zoo. He then spent over a year of his life riding that supertanker through a storm no human has ever known the likes of. You better believe Noah had a few sleepless nights puking his guts overboard, wondering if he would ever set foot on solid ground again.

Abram was called out of Ur, and sent on a nomadic safari into the rural sands of Canaan where he was repeatedly afflicted by enemies, conflict, and tragedy.

Jacob wrestled with God and man (and prevailed, Gen. 32:28). But he always limped after that.

Moses saw a miniature firestorm light up a bush, and we always think he was just a little too cowardly, a timid fellow. But I suspect Moses just knew better. He knew that little blaze was a picture of what was coming. He knew that He was being called to *be* that bush. He was being called to walk *into* the storm, to walk with the God of the Storm, the God who would bring the storm of His glory down upon him, down upon the head of the pharaoh, down upon the mountain in glory, down upon His people in judgment.

And we could go on talking about Gideon, Samson, David, Jeremiah, Ezekiel, Daniel, John the Baptist, Paul. Nobody got a desk job with a comfortable pension. Nobody got a bomb shelter. No one was ever issued a life vest. There were no parachutes. *Everyone* was harmed during the filming of each one of these movies.

We talk about "walking with God" as if that were normal, as if that were a Facebook page you could "like" and never worry about it again. But the witness of Scripture is that knowing God is dangerous, unnerving, and scandalous. Enoch walked with God, and then he just disappeared (Gen. 5:24). Elijah ended his tumultuous prophetic career riding a whirlwind of fire into heaven. Like the elders of Israel approved that stunt . . .

In part, we know that God is calling us to walk with Him in this way because life in the world He made just isn't safe. It is always fragile, brittle, on the verge of death. From the moment we inhale our first crackly gasp and cry in small, wrinkled, frowning bodies smeared with amniotic fluid and blood, to the final curtain call when we gasp our last, we are surrounded in the stormy winds. Life is but a breath. Your lungs transpose the wind into life, and then your cells—oxygen vampires—suck all the air out of the blood before returning it red to the lungs for another hit.

We don't have any control of this process. As a reminder, wind is always blowing, always gusting. We are surrounded by air, filled with breath. It's tumbling down the street. It's playing with the tops of the trees. Hair is constantly ruffled. Children are born, people wake up, words are formed by the wind strumming vocal chords, stories unfold, characters emerge and reemerge, plots and subplots intermingle and kiss and fade away and twirl in the streets like so many leaves. Life is a gale.

Which makes all our attempts to organize, all our attempts to systematize, all our attempts to structure things and run our tidy little programs, a little bit funny. This world is full of wind, it is uncertain, constantly changing directions. You don't tame the wind. It blows where it wishes. You can't tether it to your liturgy or to your filing system or to your theological charts. You don't set up "No Trespassing" signs on the coast of Florida to ward off the hurricanes. Storms don't ask for permission. The wind refuses to fill out the appropriate paper work. Life is constantly changing, and too many loved ones gone remind us that life is tenuous. White tombstones dot the landscape like post-it notes, reminding us of names and dates—and to remember life is not forever, life is short, life is uncertain. Jobs change, we lose touch with friends, sin divides, love inspires, children are born, children die, parents pass away, famines happen, economies collapse, heroes fail, victories shine. Life is always lived on the brink, on the edge. We all live on the cliffs overlooking the tossing sea. The wind blows in our faces.

Ecclesiastes says that all is *hebel*, vanity, mist, vapor, wind. But the preacher closes Ecclesiastes insisting nevertheless that there is One who shepherds the wind (Eccl. 12:11). Or better, if God is Spirit, Wind,

Breath, then God is *in* the storm, God is in the wind. He is the One blowing. He is the One breathing. It's His Word, His Voice, His Breath, His *Grace* that pushes, pulls, and upholds it all.

Jesus shows this to us most clearly. It was the Spirit-Wind that hovered over the virgin womb of Mary at His conception (Lk. 1:35). Later, the Spirit-Wind descended upon Jesus at His baptism in the form of a dove (Mk. 1:10). But this was no Hallmark moment. That wasn't a cute photo op for Jesus and a friendly bird. This was the wild dove of the worldwide flood (Gen. 8:8). This was the dove that flew in the wind that drove the waters back (Gen. 8:1). This was the dove of the Spirit that creates and re-creates worlds. And this was Jesus' official commissioning by His Father. And like the judges of old, the Spirit immediately drove Him into the wilderness to do battle with Satan (Mt. 4:1, Mk. 1:12–13). Jesus, who was and is the eternal God, was filled with the Wind of God and driven into the storm. It was the same Spirit that drove Him to carry out His mission to proclaim the gospel of the Kingdom, the good news to the poor, the new creation, the acceptable year of the Lord (Lk. 4:18–19).

Too often when someone is described as "spiritual," we think they have a halo or they are really into esoteric theology, or else they live in a monastery and speak in faint, soothing, and slightly nasal tones all the time. We think they tend to be quiet, timid, slow to move and act and speak. But "spiritual" actually means *empowered by the Spirit*. To be spiritual is not being really into meditation and incense and flickering candles. To be spiritual is to be filled with the Holy Spirit and driven to the mission of God. In that sense, the judges of Israel were spiritual men, being filled with the Spirit that drove them to do battle with new pharaohs that had arisen in Canaan (Judg. 3:10, 6:34). And perhaps Samson is the most Spirit-filled man in the entire Old Testament, though somehow I doubt any pastoral search committees would even consider his application. The Spirit came upon Samson repeatedly: inspiring him with the scandalous idea of taking a Philistine wife in order to pick a fight with the Philistines (Judg. 13:25–14:4), wrestling a lion and tearing it apart (13:6), killing thirty men and stealing their clothes (14:19), and breaking free of two new ropes to kill a thousand men (15:14–15). When the Spirit comes upon Samson, he becomes a powerful storm, carrying out God's mission for His people. But in our day, when someone gets "filled with the Spirit," the most they do is babble inarticulate words or say vague, innocuous God-stuff or (if it's in a Presbyterian church) form a new committee. Nothing scandalous or dangerous or particularly wild. Every church has its groove, everybody stays in line, people know the dress code and the acceptable buzzwords.

But even though we might think the Holy Spirit sounds sexy and kind of heroic, when it comes right down to it, this is actually why we are afraid of the grace of Jesus. His grace comes like a storm. His presence is a hurricane of glory and goodness and gladness. Literally, Genesis says that after Adam and Eve sinned, they heard the Lord God walking in the garden in the "wind of the day" (Gen. 3:8). The same Wind-Spirit that hovered over the waters at the beginning of creation comes walking in the garden, and Adam and Eve run for cover. And ever since Adam and Eve's first fig-leaf sewing party, we've grown rather adept at shelter-seeking.

The human race is basically a bunch of safety mongers and security freaks. Ever since the garden, ever since sin entered the world, we naturally run for cover. We hear the Wind coming, and we grab for foliage. We have traditional hymns and liturgies, or contemporary hymns and casual services. We have Sunday School classes and discipleship classes and community groups and Bible studies. *Quick, hide from the storm. Maybe if we make the sign of the cross like this, He won't see that we're naked. Everybody keep your head down, and maybe He won't notice us.*

But we have been filled with the rambunctious Spirit of the Triune God. He would drive us into battle. He would drive us into His new world. He would teach us to ride the wings of the Storm.

CHAPTER 13

RIDING IN THE STORM

In many ways, we are repeating ourselves. But even if it is God Himself who is the Spirit-Wind that blows over this world, there is still pain, hurt, heartache, loss. The Christian faith is not a pantheistic blender that pretends everything is God if you just take enough opium. Half of the answer is seeing God in the Storm, welcoming the Storm of His presence into our lives, and walking with God like that. But the other half of the answer is also trusting Him to hold us, to guard us, to truly keep us safe *from* the storms.

Psalm 46 says, "God is our refuge and strength, a very present help in trouble." The Psalm describes an enormous storm, a tsunami, a hurricane, with rock-slides, earthquakes, the whole world coming apart, shaking violently, nothing holding together. And in the face of that calamity, that upheaval, the psalmist sings: "There is a river whose streams make glad the city of God, the holy place of the tabernacles of the most High. God is in the midst of her, and she shall not be moved." *God is in the midst of her, and she shall not be moved.*

How is that possible? How is it possible not to be moved in the middle of a storm? How is it possible not to be moved in the middle of an earthquake? How is possible not to be moved when a hurricane bears down on your life? The psalmist says there is a peace that holds you tight in the middle of the free fall.

The psalmist says that the kind of tumult, the kind of upheaval he's talking about includes wicked men and their schemes. It includes backbiters and tyrants. It includes vindictive fathers and critical mothers. It includes false accusations and lies and abuse and scorn and betrayal. It includes political turmoil, kingdoms in disarray, terrorism, war, famine.

But God speaks into the storm. God speaks into the hurricane. God speaks into the chaos and the broken-ness, and He speaks and causes the storms to melt away, to dissolve. "He uttered his voice, the earth melted." When Miriam led the women to sing when God triumphed over the Egyptian armies in the sea, she sang of their coming triumph over the inhabitants of Canaan and proclaimed that God's great power would cause them all to melt away. *The Lord of Hosts is with us, the Lord of armies is with us, the Lord of the Exodus is with us: the God of Jacob is our refuge. Emmanuel: God with us.*

And the psalmist continues: "Come, behold the works of the Lord, what desolations He hath made in the earth. He maketh wars to cease to the ends of the earth; He breaks the bow, He cuts the spear, He burns the chariot in fire." God speaks and the threats melt away. God is a peacemaker. At His voice, wars cease, enemies are scattered, military might is broken, kingdoms are disarmed, superpowers and giants are brought down to the ground, empty and powerless. The Lord speaks into the storms and disarms them all. He does this is because He is the Lord. He made this place. He runs this place. He's the Master. And when pharaohs arise, when storms arise, when threats arise, the Lord comes for His people. The Lord speaks and makes Himself known. He speaks into the storm and brings peace to His people. He speaks and says, "Be still, and know that I am God."

One day, Jesus rode across the sea with his disciples in a boat, and a storm came upon them. These were experienced fishermen, but this was enough to scare them pretty bad. And their Master was sleeping in the hold of the boat. And they roused him and looked to him, full of fear, the boat on the verge of capsizing in the violent gale all around them. And Jesus stood and spoke into the storm. He spoke to the wind and the waves. And He said, "Peace, be still." And the wind and the waves obeyed him. And the storm melted away. And the disciples asked themselves, *Who is this? That even the wind and the waves obey Him?*

But Jesus was not done, and as soon as the boat reached the shore, another storm greeted them. There was a man who lived in the tombs in the mountains, a man whose body and soul were ravaged with an army of evil spirits. And he could not be tamed by anyone. He could not be bound. He cut himself. He was a wild beast of a man, raging, naked and fierce. And when Jesus got out of the boat, this raging storm came running to meet them. And once again, Jesus spoke to the storm. He spoke to the raging, demonic wind, and He said, "Peace, be still." And that enemy army went crashing into the sea and melted away. And when the people of that place came, they found the man clothed and in his right mind. *Who is this that even the wind and the waves obey Him?*

But Jesus still wasn't done, and a few years later, another storm broke out. A friend betrayed Him, a mob mocked and beat him, a church court lied about him, and the governor condemned him. And all the forces of evil, the principalities and powers, came down upon Him. And when it had become dark in the middle of the afternoon, when the storm could rage no louder, no fiercer, He spoke again, hanging from the cross, and this time He cried out and said, "It is finished." There was nothing more the storm could do. The storm had no more power. And he took all the shame, all the pain, all the guilt, all the anger, all the bitterness, all the lies, all the betrayal, all the abuse, all the scorn, all the loneliness, and He took it down into the ground, and He buried it deep beneath the waves of death. When he said, "It is finished," He said, "Be still." And when the centurion saw Him die, he could not help but ask who this was. And he, like the psalmist, like the Israelites, like the disciples knew the answer. There only is one answer. The One who says "be still" is the Lord of Hosts, the God of Jacob. The One who speaks into the storm is God. *Be still*, He says, *and know that I am God*. When He says *Be still*, you know that He is God because only He speaks to the storms. He's the only One whom the wind and the waves obey. He is the one who speaks peace. He is the one who makes the storms melt away. He is the one who has made peace by the blood of his cross in order to reconcile all things to Himself.

Every man, every woman, and every child in this world faces the storms of life: natural disasters, disease, sickness, divorce, betrayal, lies, sin, guilt, loneliness, fear, worry, bitterness, anger, regret, hurt too deep for words, aching down in our souls. And everyone will one day face the deep waters of death. That storm is coming, and that storm *will* overtake you. People instinctively know this. And they try to build protections for themselves. They try to make shelters from the wind. They try to build legacies. They try to pile up money and possessions. They try to build fortresses of good deeds and good intentions. But the storms will come, and they will cast everything down. And in the end death will come. Your sins and guilt will rise up like demons to drag you down to the pit forever. Your boat cannot withstand this storm.

And so that is why the only thing that matters is who is in your boat. Who is with you? The Psalmist and all those who have met Jesus cry into the storm: *The Lord of Hosts is with us; the God of Jacob is our refuge. And if God is in the midst of her, then she shall not be moved.* Our peace, our security, our hope, our safety is not found in ourselves. It is not found in our convictions. It is not found in our methods, our style, ultimately in how we feel about our circumstances, or how we explain them. Jesus is our peace. Jesus is our security. Jesus is our hope. Jesus is our refuge and strength. And there is no other.

Have you met Him? Do you know Him? Has He calmed your storm? Has He spoken into your hurricane of fears and doubts and guilt and pain? Has He said to you, "Peace, be still"? You know if He has. You know, and everyone around you knows, because there you are sitting miraculously clothed and in your right mind, and your demons have been drowned in the sea forever.

This is not just a nice thought. It would have done the disciples absolutely no good to have nice thoughts in that boat with them. It's not even enough to have nice thoughts about Jesus in your boat. It's not enough to have a theology about Jesus in your boat. It's not enough to have a liturgy that mentions Jesus, a prayer book in your boat, the latest, hippest worship song or free range, organic carrots. No, you must have Jesus in your boat. You must have the Lord of Hosts with you, the God of Jacob with you. If you don't have Jesus, you are lost and the storm will take you down. But if you have Jesus, you are safe, you are secure. If He is in the midst of you, then you shall not be moved. If Jesus is in your boat, then you are invincible, untouchable, completely impervious to every danger, every evil, every storm.

This means that life isn't dangerous in some kind of abstract, random way. Life isn't a force. Life isn't just a static state that flips on one moment and then off a few decades later. Life is not an accidental storm. Life is the spoken story of Jesus. The wind isn't accidental, either—it blows because He breathes. The storm rages because His Spirit hovers over the deep. There is One who summons up the storms, One who speaks to the storms and they obey, One who calls to us from the storms. There is One who invites us into the wind. Amos says, "For behold, He who forms mountains, and creates the wind, who declares to man what his thought is, and makes the morning darkness, who treads the high places of the earth—the Lord God of hosts is His name" (Amos 4:13).

This means that the Christian life of walking with Jesus is like riding in a boat in the Storm of the Spirit.

If you don't ever feel seasick or if all you do is strategize ways to keep everybody seated and with their seat belts fastened, something is terribly wrong. If the Spirit doesn't thrust you into battle with sin and demons and death, if you aren't routinely scared, overwhelmed, at your wits' end, then what do you need faith for? If you aren't regularly crying out to Jesus to wake up, to save you from being overwhelmed, you're not where you should be. But if you know Jesus, then you are safe, you are secure, and no storm can harm you.

CHAPTER 14

HOLDING TRUTH TOGETHER

Jesus is God, and this means He's not your pet hamster that you can bring in for show and tell. You may not pretend to put Him under a microscope and figure out how this God-thing works. You may not put Jesus into a box. You may not try to bottle His Spirit. You cannot domesticate the Christian faith and make it safe for children and respectable for primetime television. Jesus runs the universe. He is a hurricane of glory, a tornado of grace, and we are crouching on a hillside with our hang gliders waiting for the storm.

Therefore, part of obedient, Christian humility and faith is receiving gladly everything that God says in His Word. You may not pick and choose. You may not only focus on the happy parts, the sad parts, the hippie parts, or the deep philosophical parts. To follow Jesus means that we embrace all of it. We read all of Scripture, we teach all of Scripture, we preach all of Scripture, we obey all of Scripture. This is because all of Scripture is the Word of God, and therefore all of it is useful (2 Tim. 3:16–17). To the extent that men of God are not prepared for every good work, this is an indication of our failure to be trained in righteousness by every word that proceeds from the mouth of God. We have an armory fully stocked with every tactical weapon necessary to advance the cause of the gospel and engage every enemy, but sometimes we ignore whole sections of the warehouse. *All* of Scripture is the Word of Jesus, not just the red-letter bits (Lk. 24:27). We are not just "New Testament Christians." We are not Marcionites, opposing the Old and New Covenants as though they were established by different gods. We are not rationalists like Thomas Jefferson, cutting out all the hard and confusing parts of the Bible like so much origami.

From conversion to our last breath in these bodies Jesus calls us to grow up into His wisdom by holding many things together that may sometimes seem to lean apart. This is not irrationalism or to accept contradictions. But apparent tensions do tempt the faithless to let go of one end and allow one truth, one command, or one emphasis to become dominant. This biblical balance takes lots of courage because it's easier to ignore some parts of Scripture. It's easier to find a denominational stance and then just check all the boxes and keep your head down. Which means in order to embrace all of Scripture, you ultimately need the guiding and guarding of the Spirit to uphold you. But sometimes this lack of courage can actually lead one straight out of the Christian faith, riding that one-trick pony off the cliff of orthodoxy.

When I speak of apparent tensions, I'm thinking of the great doctrines: The Trinity—God is both three and one. Creation and incarnation—God is both different from what He has made and has freely entered it as a real man. God's sovereignty and man's freedom and responsibility. The great gospel indicatives that drive us to the great gospel imperatives—"this is the case because of Jesus," therefore "you must be and do this"—You are forgiven, therefore you must forgive. Like fasting and feasting, etc.

So what do we do with those?

Part of the way we faithfully receive these realities is by exploring just how big the Mission of God is. One of the ways people try to tame Jesus is by trying to keep Him inside their tiny and relatively small theological categories. If they can keep Him in their little test tubes of *ordo salutis* and other shibboleths, they feel safe and secure, and nobody needs to get hurt or misunderstand them. Of course God doesn't need us to tidy His Word up. But people still end up camping out on their favorite verses. The Calvinists camp on the sovereignty of God verses; the Arminians camp on the freedom and responsibility verses. The traditionalists hold up their "good order" verses; the revivalists point to their favorite Holy-Spirit-shazam verses. Liturgical scholars can point to the order of the sacrifices and covenant renewal and tradition for defenses of the liturgy; charismatics point to the psalms that describe worship as a holy ruckus with shouts and drums and clapping and dancing. Some Christians jump up and down on the verses about mercy and care for the poor, feeding the hungry, clothing the naked, pleading for justice on behalf of the oppressed, while others point out the commands to take dominion of the earth, to tame the animals, to study science and technology, to start businesses, or to cultivate creativity in the arts and architecture and even entertainment. As we noted as we began, Jesus says He came to make peace, and in other places He says He came to bring a sword and start fights. Or what about the fact that God speaks of the enormous blessing of the family, of marriage and children, of generational legacies . . . but Jesus says that we must give our families up, that He came to divide them, and so we must be willing to hate them? So which is it?

The point is that Jesus is Lord of all of it. Sometimes He commands us to sell everything and move to a foreign land, and sometimes He commands us to plant vineyards, dig wells, build cities, and save for our children. Sometimes He commands us to build, and sometimes He commands us to tear down. Sometimes He commands us to go to war, and sometimes He commands us to make peace. Sometimes He commands us to speak words of comfort, and sometimes He commands us to denounce, criticize, and mock. Sometimes His people meet in caves, and sometimes they meet in cathedrals. Sometimes they are called to suffer, and sometimes they are called to rule. Jesus is our Lord, our Master, our King. And we must follow Him wherever He leads.

This doesn't mean that we must not study or prioritize or seek counsel or plan or write anything down.

No, we must do all those things as we are able, seeking the face of God in prayer and Scripture to the best of our ability, but we must do everything saying, all along, "if the Lord wills" (Jas. 4:13–15). We must have Jesus. We must know Jesus. We must walk with Him. We must walk in His light. We must have His Spirit.

So, in this context, let me put in a good word for systematic theology. There is absolutely no way to avoid systematizing Scripture. Every Bible study employs some systematic theology. Every sermon is a small systematic theology. Unless you're only ever reading Scripture, you have to summarize, explain, emphasize, and harmonize, and even then, you can't read all of it all the time. Systematic theology is summarizing, explaining, emphasizing, and harmonizing, seeking to be faithful to all the contours of Scripture, and that's the necessary work of studying Scripture. That is the necessary work of being human beings with minds that are hungry to understand. As our Dutch fathers taught us, we were made to think God's thoughts after Him. This is part of what it means to be made in His image. There are better or worse systematic theologies, but in so far as systematic theology is just the rigorous, Jesus-loving study of His Word, three cheers for systematic theology.

The problems come when systematic theology is elevated to an authoritative position over the Bible, or when your theological categories are used to sandpaper inspired challenges in the text. But Jesus is Lord, not our theological categories or statement of faith. Theological categories are helpful shorthand for organizing our thoughts, and confessions of faith are helpful summaries of what the Spirit has taught us so far. But we must always remember that our thoughts are just our best attempts to describe an unending glory beyond all reckoning. We must try to describe the glory, but really, we're always tiny ants describing Mount Everest.

But this doesn't make us postmodern doubters, hiding our cowardice behind paint-by-numbers hipster authenticity. Though our knowledge may be partial, knowing Jesus means that our knowledge is nevertheless true and trustworthy. So always bearing in mind the temptation to worship the words rather than the Speaker, we nevertheless stick close to the text. The Words of God are sweet to us, they are honey, they are strength and wisdom and glory. We want the word of God to dwell inside of us richly, and so we sing it and chant it and recite it and memorize it and teach it (Col. 3:16). Since we've been born again by the incorruptible seed of the Word of God (which lives forever), we are like newborn babies starving for more, longing for the pure milk of the word (1 Pet. 1:23–2:3). But we also confess that God wants us to grow up into maturity and understanding systematically. He wants us to exercise our senses and dig into the meat of wisdom (Heb. 5:13–14)—because once we've tasted His grace, we can't get enough.

CHAPTER 15

COLLISION COURSE
WITH GLORY

Again and again, the Scriptures remind us to continue the way we started: in the grace of the forgiveness of Jesus and the power of His Spirit (Gal. 3:3, Col. 2:6). Christians never grow out of the grace of forgiveness. They never strike out on their own. They always cling to cross. They always walk in the Spirit. But this is part of the clue for the blueprints of our obedience to Jesus and His mission. The beginning of our walk with Jesus is a new birth: *regeneration.* But this new life is not merely something that happens to *us,* as it turns out. It includes us individually, but when we look at what God says about our "rebirth," in Scripture, it quickly becomes apparent it's a lot bigger than you and me. The only time Jesus uses the word "regeneration," He's talking about the New World of the Kingdom of God—when He sits on the throne of His glory with the twelve apostles judging the twelve tribes of Israel (Mt. 19:28). In other words, when Jesus uses the word "regeneration," He's talking about something cosmic, political, and global. He's talking about the beginning of the New Heavens and the New Earth, the whole world reborn through the work of the Spirit at Pentecost, the New Eon, the New Era of the Kingdom, and its culmination when the end comes and all things are delivered up to the Father (1 Cor. 15:24).

So the redemption accomplished in the life, death, and resurrection of Jesus is global, cosmic, universal, more thorough than anything our little brains can even begin to imagine. It extends to economics and foreign policies, science and nutrition, technology and space exploration, and much more. And when we zoom in on the question of individual salvation, don't think for a moment that we're leaving that big picture behind. In fact, we're talking about the same thing. This is why the New Testament talks about the gift of the Holy Spirit to men and women and children as the down payment, the first fruits, the guarantee of the inheritance, the beginning of what will become of the nations, the world, the universe (Rom. 8:22–23, Eph. 1:13–14).

This is worth jumping up and down on for a bit: The same Spirit that rushes down upon people and drives them to carry out the mission of Jesus—war with sin, death, and Satan—is simultaneously and through those very same people renewing all of creation. In theological categories, we're talking about the parallel between soteriology and eschatology. Eschatology is the doctrine of the end times. Soteriology is the doctrine of salvation.

Within soteriology, sanctification is the word we use to describe how the Holy Spirit impresses the life and gifts of Jesus more and more into the lives of sinners, filling them and driving them to glad obedience, cheerful sacrifice, and bold warfare. After Jesus commands dead people to live, and they begin to trust and obey Him, they always necessarily grow up into Him and they resemble Him more and more. And this is why the world cannot go unaffected. This is why soteriology must drive our eschatology. In both soteriology and eschatology we are talking about ends, goals, and mission. And the final step of our sanctification will occur at the resurrection in our glorification, when even our mortal body is glorified and becomes like the body of Jesus forever (1 Cor. 15:49). The bodies and lives of all who belong to Jesus are on a collision course with the glory of God. Nothing good will be lost.

But the mission of the Spirit is not just about individuals and the world; it's also about the Church (ecclesiology). To be born again means to be born into a new family. Regeneration means you have a new father. Adam was your dad by the flesh. The Devil was your dad spiritually, because, before you met Jesus, you wanted to obey the voice of the serpent. When you were in your sins, you loved death, and you were an enemy of God (Rom. 5:10, Col. 1:21) But when you were made alive, when you were born again, God became your Father forever and you joined His family—those who do His will (Mt. 12:50). In fact, Jesus' promise of the Holy Spirit is specifically so that we will not be left as orphans (Jn. 14:8). The Holy Spirit is alone what gives us the audacity to call God our Dad (Rom. 8:14–17) and to join enthusiastically with His building project.

But the cornerstone of this magnificent building (i.e., the Church) is Jesus, the stone of stumbling, the stone which the builders rejected (1 Pet. 2:7). And here we come to our warning again: The builders are the Bible study leaders, the worship leaders, the pastors and elders and deacons, the seminary students and missionaries and mercy workers. He is often most offensive to the very people who think they understand, who think they've figured it out. But Jesus remains Lord, and we remain servants. He loves us, but He doesn't need us. He can raise up children to Abraham from a pile of stones left at the edge of the Jordan River (a reminder from another time when He dispensed of a generation of unbelievers). He doesn't need our flyer campaigns, our hip and trendy church names, our buildings, our books, our conferences, our theological explanations, our traditions. He's free to use any of it, all of it, some of it, none of it, whenever and however He pleases. He is the Lord, He is the Master Builder. And He knows what He's doing.

The prophet Daniel caught a glimpse of the plans in a dream centuries before Jesus even showed up. Nebuchadnezzar saw a statue, a man made of different kinds of metals, representing the ancient empires that would rise and fall, but then a stone, cut out without hands struck the statue in the feet and the image collapsed, crumbling into dust and carried away by the wind (Dan. 2:31–35). But the stone that struck the statue grew into a great mountain and filled the whole earth. That mountain is the Kingdom of God which shall never be destroyed, but shall break in pieces and consume all the kingdoms of the earth (Dan. 2:44). Daniel's dream matches what Jesus said right before He ascended into heaven. He gave us our marching orders: All authority in heaven and on earth had been given to Him as His possession and inheritance, and He sent us to announce that good news to every creature, every nation, every president, every slave, every sleazy politician, every blue-collar worker, everybody (Mk. 16:15, cf. Ps. 2:6–9). We're to make them all disciples by baptizing them in the Triune Name and teaching them to submit to the words of King Jesus in everything (Mt. 28:18–20).

That's our task, our Great Commission, and Paul says in 1 Corinthians that Jesus must reign until every enemy has been put down, the last enemy being death itself (1 Cor. 15:25–26). That's our glimpse of the future: the Kingdom of Jesus will be proclaimed throughout the earth until every knee bows and every tongue confesses allegiance to the name of Jesus, to the glory of God the Father (Phil. 2:10–11). In other words, the history of the world will be the rebirth of the world as surely as Jesus rose from the dead. The universe will be raised up from the curse of sin, the shadows will be driven away, light and life will reign forever. Science will bow the knee to Jesus, technology will praise Jesus, economics will confess that Jesus is Lord, and all of politics will acknowledge that He is King. Russia will bow the knee to Jesus. China will bow the knee to Jesus. Columbia will bow the knee to Jesus. One day America will repent of her sin and fall down and worship Jesus. Who knows what our geopolitical landscape will look like, who knows what names they will bear—but they will all come and walk in the light of the Lamb and bring their glory and honor before Him (Rev. 21:24).

From one angle, we can look across the ages and see the Spirit poured out at Pentecost hovering over the world, slowly blowing, roaring over the chaos and darkness, raising up pastors and priests, kings and nobles, slaves and prostitutes. The Sunrise from on High has visited us; it's getting lighter out every minute, every day (Lk. 1:78, Eph. 5:8–14). But when we watch the particular stories of nations, generations, families, individuals, the shadows don't just disappear—they seem to meander, they seem to curl and spin, like watching one of those high speed stop-action sequences on a nature show. The shadows even seem to crawl in the wrong direction at times. But an imperishable seed has been planted. That seed was the body of Jesus that went into the ground, and on the third day burst up in light and life that can never die. That same life and light was poured out at Pentecost, and that imperishable seed exploded, sending the infectious shrapnel of grace to the ends of the earth by the preaching of the gospel. But it isn't good enough to say that Jesus wins, and who cares about the details. The announcement that Jesus wins means that Jesus conquers sin. Jesus conquers death. Jesus frees the slaves. Jesus destroys the wicked. Jesus forgives sinners. And in order for this to be the end of the story, it must fill every page of the story.

People are conquered by Jesus. Individuals are conquered by Jesus. And Jesus wins them. Jesus becomes their King. Jesus washes them clean. Jesus chases the shadows out of individuals as surely as He is bidding the shadows flee this world. And this is why soteriology and eschatology go hand in hand. Remember: Jesus is Lord, and we are not. Jesus is not waiting for us. Jesus is not wringing His hands in heaven wishing He could do something to help. Jesus is King of this world because the kingdoms of this world have become the kingdoms of our Lord and of His Christ (Rev. 11:15). And our King is leading the conquest of this world. He purchased the ends of the earth with His precious blood, and therefore it all belongs to Him. He has declared war on it all, and therefore when Jesus claims possession of an individual formally at the moment of his baptism, that is fundamentally a declaration of war on the old man. And either he will cling to his old man and go down to destruction broken to pieces like a potter's vessel with all of God's enemies, or he will cling to the sword that slays him and be raised to new life. There is no third option. Jesus always gets His man.

The Spirit blows where He wishes. We don't bind Him. We don't tame Him. And God will have plenty of surprises, plenty of jokes that will make our bellies ache with laughter and our cheeks shine with happy tears. There are piles of mystery, piles of hard cases, but we can cheerfully leave all of those to Jesus, keep working faithfully at the mission He has given, and wait expectantly for the punch line on the last day. But in the mean time, we have God's normal, obvious, manifest goodness. The children of God and the children of the devil are as obvious as the nose on your face (Gal. 5:19–24). Nothing really that mysterious about it. The good guys and the bad guys pretty much wear uniforms, John says (1 Jn. 3:8–10). They either love Jesus, love to obey Him, and love His people, or they don't. It's pretty simple.

And all of that is to say that people who know Jesus are as different from people who don't know Jesus as the old world will be to the new. Of course, we await the resurrection of our bodies. Our old, creaking, broken bodies constantly remind us of the old world, but we are being renewed day by day in the inner man (2 Cor. 4:16). We have this treasure in earthen vessels, rotting nations, rebellious pottery, but it's a treasure that cannot be lost because Jesus is born again, and now, so are we.

And this means the Word of God is a fire in a Christian's soul. You can't have this imperishable seed get a hold of you and leave you unchanged. People who know Jesus, who have been taken up into the Storm of His Spirit, are driven people, confident people, the most courageous people in the whole world. People who have been conquered by the grace of Jesus have nothing to lose and everything to gain. The world belongs to their King, and they cannot rest until they see it conquered. Conquered people are a conquering people.

CHAPTER 16

SEEKER INSENSITIVE

If our worship of idols is our central problem, then true worship of the true God must be at the center of our repentance. While Christians give thanks and rejoice and worship Jesus always, since the beginning there has been a special emphasis on the weekly gathering to hear the Word read and explained and to celebrate the meal that Jesus gave us.

One of the most important things to notice about the early chapters of Revelation is the fact that John meets with Jesus in a vision on the Lord's Day (Sunday), and what John witnesses is a heavenly worship service (Rev. 1:10, chs. 4–11). Paul says that we who are in Christ have ascended into heaven with Him, and therefore our worship takes place united to Jesus by His Spirit (Eph. 2:6, Heb. 12:18–29). But perhaps what is most crucial about John's vision is not merely that he sees our worship joined to the heavenly worship, but he sees the effects of our heavenly worship on the earth. When the Lamb is worshiped, the seals are opened (Rev. 4–7). When the prayers of the saints arise to God like incense, angels blow trumpets and judgments fall on the earth (Rev. 8).

And so, if we live in a culture that is crumbling, with leaders blaspheming and actively seeking to legislate immorality and folly, one of the questions we ought to ask is what is our worship doing? Or better, what is our worship *not* doing? When the first disciples met together to hear the word and break bread, the word of God spread like wildfire through the cities of Jerusalem, Judea, Samaria, to the ends of the earth. When God's people meet together in the name of Jesus in the power of the Spirit around the Word and the Meal, it should be explosive. Sins should be confessed and forgiven, enemies reconciled, truth proclaimed boldly to wicked rulers, in short, there should be radical healing and radical collisions with the enemies of grace. When Jesus is worshiped rightly, many should be drawn to the light, and it should bring the sons of light into direct conflict with the children of darkness.

From the beginning of the Church, a fairly straightforward pattern developed for the gatherings of Christians with the reading and explaining of Scripture, singing of psalms and hymns, the prayers of the people, offerings, and the celebration of the Lord's Supper, the sharing of bread and wine. This basic pattern can be found in all Christian traditions throughout the world. At my church, this looks like a very traditional liturgy: we sing historic hymns and psalms and canticles and chants, we have a hearty appreciation for the Church calendar, orienting our time to the life of Jesus as our fathers before us. Some of our more enthusiastic missional brothers might go so far as to call us seeker-insensitive.

Given everything we have covered thus far, it might seem odd to defend the legitimacy of a historically leaning, Bible-saturated, Spirit-filled formal worship that is recognizably traditional in the sense that it gladly draws from the songs and prayers and orders of the historic Church. Isn't "traditional" synonymous with "dead," and doesn't "liturgy" rhyme with "liberal"? In what follows, I want to sketch a way of loving the deep roots of the Christian tradition. And I'll show why loving Christian tradition in this way is not at all at odds with but is actually one of the greatest sources for living out the radical, rambunctious life of Christ. At the same time, given the days we live in, I want to make it clear that I'm making a case for a traditional *evangelical* worship, or a historic *Protestant* worship. In other words, nothing said here should be understood as cozying up to Roman Catholicism or Eastern Orthodoxy, two branches of the Christian Church with important contributions to the body of Christ and with which I have many significant concerns.

But that said, and beginning with the obvious, the Church didn't just get started in the last fifty years. And the Church doesn't need to be reinvented every decade. The Church has been around for two thousand years, which means that Jesus has been conquering the world and gathering treasures into His temple for two thousand years. Worship that doesn't participate in that legacy misses out on the story that we are part of. And not to put too fine a point on it, the biblical case for leaning into this legacy is the fifth commandment: *Honor your father and mother.* It's not an accident that as the Church began rejecting its own fathers and mothers, our children learned the lesson and started doing the same.

So what does the Bible actually say about worship?
The Bible says that "traditional" worship is warfare.
We see this in the Old Testament when Abraham built
altars throughout Canaan—like bombing runs prepar-
ing the land for the conquest that Joshua would carry
out centuries later (e.g., Gen. 12:8, Josh. 8). When God
brought down Jericho, He did it through the joyful
shouts of praise of His people (Josh. 6). Jehoshaphat
sent the choir out in front of the army to sing praises,
and the Lord set ambushes for the enemies of Judah
(2 Chr. 20:20–22). David even sang about the power
of praise as being like a sword in the hands of God's
people, executing vengeance on the nations and pun-
ishments on the peoples (Ps. 149). When saints sing
their hearts out God sends judgments on the earth.
And lest we think this was all just an Old Covenant
thing, Hebrews says that everything is amped up in
the New Covenant. Now we are not merely come to
an earthly mountain that shakes and smokes, we are
come to Mount Zion, the city of the living God, the
heavenly Jerusalem, to an innumerable company of
angels (Heb. 12:22–25). And when we draw near to
this heavenly city, this Mount Zion, what is God doing?
He's shaking heaven and earth in order to remove all
of those things that can be shaken (Heb. 12:26–27).

We are receiving a kingdom that *cannot* be shaken, and so God comes as a consuming fire, burning up the chaff and purifying the gold.

The Bible says that, while Christian always have access to the Father through Jesus, in worship there is a special and unique experience of God's presence. Christians acknowledged this by meeting on the first day of the week in specific commemoration of the resurrection of Jesus (Jn. 20:1, 19, 26, Acts 2:1, 20:7, 1 Cor. 16:2, Rev. 1:10). Jesus keeps coming to meet with His people on the first day of the week, and then the Spirit of Jesus comes on Pentecost, another Sunday, another Easter, when the disciples of Jesus are gathered together for prayer. And just as Jesus revealed Himself by explaining the Scriptures and in the breaking of the bread on that first Easter to the disciples going to Emmaus (Lk. 24:13–35), so too, after He ascended back into heaven, His followers continue to meet weekly to hear their Lord in the public reading of the Scriptures and to recognize their Lord in the breaking of bread together, on the first day of the week (Acts 20:7).

The Bible says that Christian worship is sacrificial. Going back to tabernacle and temple, God has always been approached through sacrifice. Sacrifice points to the need for the shedding of blood to take away sin (Heb. 9:22). Sacrifice points to communion through the meals that were shared in God's presence (Exod. 24:11, Lev. 7:11–15). Sacrifice points to the way God is determined to receive us by His grace as we are but also how He refuses to leave us the way we are. When a worshiper draws near to God in worship, he leans his hands on the head of the animal, confessing his sins and identifying with that animal (Lev. 1:4). Then the animal is killed and cut into pieces and arranged on the fire on the altar (Lev. 1:5–9). Paul exhorts the Romans to offer their bodies as living sacrifices, which is their reasonable priestly service (or liturgy). He is saying that as we offer our bodies in worship and obedience to Christ, God is transforming us from glory to glory. Sacrifice points to the way God takes us and cuts us and transforms us through the cleansing and testing fire of His Spirit until we become a sweet-smelling aroma in His presence. Sacrifice ultimately points to Jesus, who is the end of all bloody sacrifice, but who also fulfills all of the sacrifices. In Him, we offer the sacrifice of praise to God continually, the fruit of our lips, giving thanks to His name (Heb. 13:15).

This is why many have noted that different parts of the traditional worship service roughly correspond to the main three sacrifices: the sin offering, the ascension offering (whole burnt), and the peace offering. In Jesus, we draw near and confess our sins and are assured of forgiveness (sin offering). In Jesus, we ascend into the heavenly places to Mount Zion where we are transformed by the Word read and proclaimed from glory to glory (ascension offering). Finally, we sit down to feast with the Lord like the elders of Israel of old on Mount Sinai. We eat bread and drink wine in peace because our sins are forgiven, and we have been made kings and priests to our God (peace offering).

At the same time, certain kinds of religious people love to hide from Jesus in religious forms. And one of the reasons traditional forms give so many people the heebie-jeebies is because so many satanic-zombies run the old programs. There's a good reason why organs and robes and cathedrals are good props and settings for horror movies: in many cases, the Spirit of Jesus hasn't showed up there for a few decades or more. And when a culture crumbles and the Church is crumbling along with it, people grab for whatever looks solid. And plenty of people who were hiding from Jesus in contemporary worship services can hop over to more traditional forms and feel like they're just as inoculated to grace. So in my enthusiasm and support for the traditional Biblical forms, I want to do everything I can to scare away the groupies and posers. In our eagerness to recover the treasures of the past, in our eagerness to ditch the shallow spontaneity of the modern church (because it's hard for most people to be brilliant and deep on the fly), we must watch out for the ditches we are veering toward. In other words, in my neck of the woods we aren't in danger of having our congregation doing hand motions in the aisles to "Father Abraham" or "This Little Light of Mine." Though there are plenty of churches with rock bands and strobe lights and smoke machines doing their thing, when you've grown weary and frustrated with that kind of pathetic, it is sometimes tempting to send all the troops to that side of the battlefield to fight that temptation when it's probably the least vulnerable position on the field by that point.

In other words, as soon as you obey Jesus, study the issues, pray for wisdom, seek counsel, and then implement a plan, you are immediately in danger of becoming a Pharisee. This isn't an argument against implementing a plan or praying for wisdom or any of that stuff—it's just the standard warning that comes on the bottle. As soon as you think you know what you're doing, you run the risk of thinking that you know what you're doing. But the answer to that danger is not doubting or putting on a faux-humility. The answer is *gratitude*. Thankfulness is actually what is at the center of all true worship of Jesus. When we hear the Word of the Good News of Jesus, above all else, it makes us thankful. And when we break the bread and share the wine, it's our enactment of thanksgiving, which is why the early church called it the Eucharist (*eucharisteo* means "I give thanks"). When you're thankful, you receive the gifts of God, and you remain teachable. Humility obeys, and the humble give thanks for obedience.

Biblical worship should have recognizable results, filling people with an unstoppable joy, driving them to confess and repent of sin, love and forgive their neighbors, to minister to those who are hurting and those in need. But there is a key middle step in the process, which is frequently hard to distinguish from its counterfeits. That key middle step is an authentic, Spirit-filled walk with God. And we really do struggle with words at this point because God is free to meet us in a plethora of ways, and sometimes we really only notice what was actually going on in the rear-view mirror. It might be during a sermon, it might be at a baptism, it might be during the liturgy, it might be in a Bible study, it might be when your parents confront you about sin in your life, in might be when your wife tells you she slept with another man, it might be when you confess your long standing porn habit to your wife, it might be when your child dies unexpectedly, or in a quiet moment driving alone in the car. And most likely it's at millions of tiny points in our lives that we don't even realize. Because Jesus loves us and keeps His covenant promises to us, He freely meets with us to manifest His power and presence to us in many different ways. But—and this is the point—*we must insist that this happen*. We must know Jesus. We must meet with this Jesus. We must walk with this Jesus. We must have His Spirit at work in our lives. Dead religion, stale tradition, pharisaic hypocrisy, is the easiest thing to produce. It springs up like ugly on Lady Gaga.

In every tradition, the sign of the Spirit's absence is the fact that people's lives are unchanged, unaffected, and untransformed by the powerful working of the Spirit of God and worldliness creeps in. Therefore, faithful shepherds must look for the evidence of the Spirit's presence in transformed lives, in abounding fruitfulness, in unexpected grace. If worship is war, if worship is the arming of the troops, the aerial warfare of the Spirit, we should pray for evidence that the campaign is going forth. We should pray for results. We should pray for the fire of the Spirit to fall. It is not enough to have a solid biblical theology of worship. It's not enough to draw the formula up on the board and explain that the Spirit in fact *must* be present. Yes, but *is* the Spirit actually there with you?

CHAPTER 17

RULES ARE LIKE RABBITS

Let's say Jesus shows up in a big way, the Spirit comes down like the wild storm of grace that He is, and reformation and revival break out. People are gathering to worship Jesus, listening to His Word and sharing His Meal as the community of the New World of the Spirit. One of the key teachings of Jesus that we would need to proclaim up and down and side to side, over and over, would be the doctrine of *justification by faith*. We know this first of all because that's what Paul filled the pages of his letters with. That's not an accident. The Spirit that inspired Paul to write knew full well that what Paul and the first disciples of Jesus faced, would be central to the story of the Church throughout the ages. The Spirit knew we needed this. The New Testament isn't just a historical curiosity.

For Paul, justification had everything to do with who Jesus really was, and therefore what it means to be in *that* Jesus, to know *Him*, to walk with *Him*. In other words, what it means to be a Christian. However, some of the Jews who believed in Jesus said that in order to be really part of God's family, non-Jews had to be circumcised and keep the Old Testament ceremonial laws. These people were called Judaizers. That sounds bad now, but be assured that the Judaizers were the conservatives, the Bible scholars, the respected teachers and professors. And if you think about it, it shouldn't be too hard to sympathize with them. Everybody gravitates toward seat belts and rules. Everybody's worried about being misunderstood, misjudged, or accused. So we want safety nets, bullet proof vests, impervious material between us and danger. The world is a windy place, it lurches unexpectedly, and we want to tie everything down. That's actually pretty reasonable if you're human. But Jesus can take a nap during a storm, and this freaks us out. It looks like He doesn't care.

For the Judaizers, it was a matter of keeping things clean, organized, tidy, and safe. One of the old ways God had kept things simple in the Old Covenant was by making Israel a separate people from the other nations, specifically through circumcision and the purity codes. But part of the good news of Jesus was that all those laws were fulfilled in Him, and now *all* nations were invited to be His people. On the one hand, those laws were talking about the perfection and purity of Jesus, so if you know Jesus, now you are clean, and you are a full member of His family by faith in His finished work on your behalf. Now Jesus is our holiness code. He is our purity accomplished, and His life is the shape of the holiness we strive for. But the law also pointed out and revealed the imperfection and impurity of all men, the impossibility of perfection, even and especially for Jews. The law was a standing proclamation of the curse of sin. This is because no one ever had kept it perfectly, and blemishes and uncleanness show up everywhere for everyone no matter how scrupulous they are (Gal. 3:10).

Laws and rules and codes and traditions can feel safe. They offer a form of security so that you feel like you know what to expect, what to do, and what to say. But life's not really like that. Sin is never that simple.

The law can't deal with all the complexities of life. It can't handle all the exigencies of human experience. It can't take away our sins. It can't make us clean. Laws just point out the dirt, the failures, the injustice.

And this is why rules are like rabbits: their gestation period is wicked fast if you trust in them. What Jesus brought was an end to that old way of dealing with sin and evil in the world. The law is a deterrent, and consequences do discourage evil men. But the law isn't the answer. Rules don't fix people, and often they just aggravate the problem. The Spirit of Jesus is the answer to the problem of the messiness of life. The Spirit is the Wisdom of God that embeds the righteousness of God in human beings—the ninja ability needed to walk through this world skillfully.

But the reason why we want rules instead of the Spirit is because we *want* to be right, we *don't* want to be wrong, and we want to *make sure* all along the way. We are all security freaks, and we want constant reassurance that we're OK, everything's going to be OK, that we won't be wrong, that we won't be ashamed in the end. We're like little kids constantly looking up, checking people's faces to see if we have everybody's approval.

But there are at least two problems with this. First, we are sinners who have been wrong, and we will certainly be wrong again. And second, nothing but Jesus can save us from ourselves or all the things that can and do go wrong. But this is why these questions have everything to do with justification—with *being right*. This is why Paul spent so much time and energy and ink repeating again and again: the just shall live by faith in Jesus; righteousness is by trusting in Jesus; the only way we can always be safe from every accusation is by Jesus alone.

So even though that original controversy has died and actual Judaizers are an extinct species (mostly) in our day, Christians ever since have been tempted to add to Jesus. You need Jesus *and this one other thing* to keep you safe: Jesus plus theology, Jesus plus social justice, Jesus plus emotional experiences, Jesus plus science, Jesus plus being cool. People even turn the gifts of God into those badges of assurance (Bible reading, quiet time, sacraments, etc.), and usually people find safety in community. This is why justification is always a fellowship and membership issue (e.g., Gal. 2:11–16).

However, this is fundamentally morality by democracy. This is justification by votes. This is the righteousness of man, which is always faulty, unstable, and, ironically, infamously *unjust*. We think if certain people approve us—vindicate us—we will be safe, secure, and unashamed. But Jesus proved this absolutely, completely, utterly wrong. And He did that by being absolutely right in every way humanly possible . . . and then the justice of man miscarried, right on schedule. The justice of man was unmasked for the sham that it is: a bloodthirsty mob. Every man is a Cain, a murderer, a hater, a self-serving bastard. We think we are safe in the crowd, in the herd, wearing the uniform, keeping our heads down, conforming. But it turns out we're conforming to death. We're justifying failure with more failure. We're defending the stench by pointing out that everyone else smells the same way, *and besides, some people really like it.*

But Jesus came to break the power of herds. Jesus came to bring God's truth about us, our world, and His goodness. Which is why we're still talking about justification and the age-old heresy of Judaizing. It started off with Jews following Jesus: they could not believe that God would stop requiring complete keeping of the law as part of their full membership status. *Surely, the followers of Jesus still had to be circumcised! Surely they had to keep the kosher food laws and refrain from trimming the sides of their beards!* But what Jesus lived and taught implicitly, and the apostles proclaimed freely, is that

Jesus is the end of the law for all who believe. *Jesus is enough.* It's not Jesus plus sacrifice. It's not Jesus plus circumcision. And therefore it's not even Jesus plus baptism or Jesus plus the Lord's Supper or prayer or organic popsicles. The Protestant Reformation slogan of "Christ Alone" was this original war cry, the defiant, joyful shout of every true revival of the gospel, insisting from the bottom of souls made free, that what Jesus accomplished in His life, death, and resurrection is complete freedom, joy, forgiveness, justice, and acceptance. And we receive this freedom in history, in our bodies, in communities, *by faith*—by believing God. And it is the pleasure and glory of God for this freedom and forgiveness and justice to then permeate our circumstances and transfigure all of the details of every moment, such that Jesus is living in and through us in all things by the Holy Spirit.

And this has everything to do with telling the truth and fighting sin. Paul reserves some of his most lethal invective for Judaizers. He calls the circumcision party such unflattering names as dogs, mutilators of the flesh, and at one point suggests they get sloppy with their scalpels (Phil. 3:2). He calls their so-called gospel a "different gospel" and "another gospel" and has no problem telling the Galatians that people who preach this false gospel are damned to Hell (Gal. 1:6–9). God damn anyone who preaches another gospel than the free, supernatural grace proclaimed by Paul.

We live in a world full of lies, and we are so used to hearing lies and speaking lies that the truth comes like a bucket of cold water, shocking and offensive. Jesus says that the truth sets people free—so if we live in a culture of slaves (and we do), then we are clearly a culture full of lies. In other words, the safety that we seek in the approval of men and the security we seek in badges of conformity are actually a form of slavery. We are enslaved to the opinions of men, slaves of our fears, afraid of being wrong, afraid of sin, of pain, of shame, of being embarrassed, of getting sick, of dying. And we are slaves of pleasure because most of our addictions are just covers for our cowardice and insecurity and fear.

And this explains why there can be so many professing Christians in the West who are so embarrassingly impotent. We are churches full of Judaizers who have taken Paul's advice and castrated ourselves. How are we Judaizers? We have abandoned the gospel of Christ *alone*. We have added to the Word of God. It's Jesus plus liturgy, Jesus plus icons, Jesus plus organic food, Jesus plus football, Jesus plus pleasure, Jesus plus respectability, Jesus plus beer, Jesus plus being cool, Jesus plus classical Christian education, Jesus plus Reformed theology, whatever.

And the point isn't that Jesus doesn't like any of those things. Rather, it's that Jesus knows none of those things are strong enough *by themselves* to guard your heart and mind. To add anything to Jesus is always to dilute Him. And ultimately, that is to scorn His grace and blood. And Paul says God damn that. Did you begin by the Spirit and now will you continue by the flesh (Gal. 3:3)? Do you really want the justice of man? The strength of man is flimsy. It careens from ditch to ditch, from extreme to extreme driven by the whims of drunken fools. And this is why it doesn't make you bold or free or even safe. It only makes slaves and cowards, pretenders and hypocrites.

Every *thing* we hold on to is an idol. And every son of Adam is a natural idolater. As Calvin insisted, the human heart is an idol factory, churning out fetishes and figurines without any effort. But idolatry is never just an unfortunate dead end. Idolatry is never a harmless misunderstanding. Idolatry is at its heart an insane murderous terrorism. Idolatry tears people and communities apart, leaving the disfigured, dysfunctional, deaf, blind, and maimed behind (Ps. 115:4–8).

Trusting an idol is like playing horseshoes with land mines. Idolatry leaves the image of God defaced.

But when we tell the truth about idols, we set men free. When we repent of our own idols, we begin to become the human beings we were created to be. When we point out the idolatry in obsessing over health food, or finding hope in alternative fads, or finding our identity in theological gnat-strangling or liturgical costume parties—when we do this, we will be hated, maligned, and misunderstood. But when the idols finally come down, people wake up, slaves are set free, and cowards become bold, because now they have the invincible justice of God in Christ.

CHAPTER 18

NOT AFRAID ANYMORE

One of our current cultural buzzwords is "authenticity." But so much of our discussion about it is an obvious and sickening scam, because it begins in the wrong place. Our generation (like many others) has gone terribly wrong. And we know this down in our bones. We have contributed to the wrong in this world, and that is why we are so insecure about whether we are being "authentic" or not (more on this in a bit). This is why people do all kinds of ridiculous things to try to fix the gnawing in their souls: they try to be popular, successful, rich, sexy, healthy, respected, feared . . . But we're just trading idols: we're just moving the mold to a different room in the house. This is salvation by carving a piece of creation (job, beauty, money, etc.). We may be failures, we may be guilty, we may be foolish, we may make mistakes, we may be overweight, we may be ugly— but at least we have friends! at least we wear the right clothes! at least we have a membership at the gym! at least we celebrate our oddity, our perversion, our dysfunction, by hanging out with other people who have the same problem! In other words, this is authenticity by self-justification, by the justice of man. But everybody still ends up buried in the ground. And none of those friends can keep your heart beating. None of the smiles can keep your skin from wrinkling. None of those clubs can prevent cancer or Alzheimer's. We need a better source of authenticity.

This is why the answer to all insecurity and all failure is Jesus. Jesus is your righteousness. If you're worried about sin you committed—Jesus bled and died for that sin. If you're worried about sin committed against you—Jesus suffered in agony for that sin. You don't have to be bitter. If you're worried about being a loser, left out, lonely, never getting married, never having children—Jesus was rejected, ignored, hated, despised, spat upon, and became a profane joke because of His love for you. If your identity is in Jesus, then you are not missing anything. Maybe faithfulness and obedience will mean being hated, rejected, and being a little lonelier for a time, but Jesus endured the same darkness—and far worse—in His great love for you. Are you afraid of letting your parents or your friends down? Jesus is your vindication before God and the whole world. Whatever lies, whatever failures, and whatever face-plants, God is going to stand up on the last day and boast about you. He's going to brag about His love for you and His grace in you. You are not damaged goods. You are holy, blameless, pure, undefiled, completely and utterly righteous because of the blood of the Lamb. We can live like everything is right because it is and it will be.

This is why the quest for authenticity is all about justification. Those who set off on quests to "find themselves" can only do so under two possible scenarios. The first found themselves when they were found by Jesus. And when they were found, it was like looking into a mirror for the first time and laughing at how silly they looked. These people who have been found by Jesus (and subsequently have found themselves) set off on the quest for authenticity like a child digging through a toy box looking for his favorite action figure, his favorite hat, his favorite stick. It's all joy and gladness and gratitude. They go looking for themselves like a game of hide-and-seek. They are like G.K. Chesterton's character, Innocent Smith, who traveled the world in search of his own house, chasing his own favorite hat, and wooing his own wife multiple times under different names just for the fun of it.

The only other quest for authenticity is the one for those who are still lost. They are looking for themselves because they have not been found. These lost souls have no favorite hats because they didn't know they had any. They have no favorite sticks because they were never handed one. They are orphans, homeless and fatherless, and they have nothing in this world. And they band together like alley cats in dysfunctional communities, always glued together with common fears, insecurities, and enemies.

But in Jesus, God comes to us, to be the Father of all the fatherless, the Defender of orphans in their distress, and the Finder of the all lost sheep. All things belong to Him, and if they belong to Jesus, they belong to His people: The universe is our sandbox, our toy box, our backyard. We know the difference between being really lost in a real wood and being lost in the whirling universe of a backyard with a wild imagination all afternoon.

If the Church is doing her job, proclaiming this good news of forgiveness and justice in Jesus, then she ought to attract people who need that forgiveness and that justice. A faithful church ought to attract tax collectors and sinners and prostitutes and homosexuals. A faithful church ought to attract the broken, the despised, the rejected, the hurting. And they'll come in off the street with all their addictions, all their pain, all their confusion, and they'll puke on the sanctuary carpet from time to time and need to sleep off their hangovers in the pastor's office. And praise God for that. But Jesus doesn't leave us where He finds us. Where rottenness and thorns once grew, the fruit of the Spirit begins to emerge. And when someone gets a new heart, they start to glorify their life with beautiful things, and they start to adorn the temple of their body, the temple of their home, and the temple of their family with glory. Jesus puts His glory in our hearts so that it can spill out into all of life. And the glory of Jesus is full of diversity and multiplicity and wonderful differences, and the Spirit turns it all into harmony.

This brings us full circle to the quest for authenticity and justification. Justification is the doctrine of play. It means all is right with you, and God, and the world. It means you live your life in the backyard of the universe, and you have all afternoon. In Christ, all things are yours, all things are free, and all things are given. You have nothing to prove, nothing to lose, no one to fear.

But there are some who come into the church who have not yet shaken their craven, orphan ways. They grasp at sticks and toys and stuff them in their pockets, looking suspiciously at everyone around them. Or maybe they put on grand shows, displaying their sticks and action figures, their free range chickens and their raw organic milk, their theological prowess and their liturgical engineering expertise, winking and nodding, hoping that everyone will respect them now (not realizing that everyone else has been given sticks and action figures too, and Jesus owns all the chickens and milk and theology). Usually you can tell the lost souls by the way they worry all the time about what other people might be misunderstanding.

But when the lost sons and daughters are found and adopted and clothed and given their inheritance, the Father throws a party with loud music and dance. It brings peace, a radical, overflowing peace like a lazy Sunday afternoon, like a stream running along merrily in the forest. It's a peace that passes all understanding. Those who have been found by their God are always found, always *being* found, like an epic game of hide and seek, laughing with their God and Father.

CHAPTER 19

HOLY WAR

When we know the real Jesus, what can separate us from the love of God in Christ Jesus our Lord? The resounding answer is *nothing* (Rom. 8:35). This is the only solid, biblical basis for waging our war with sin, Satan, death, and all evil. When people meet Jesus, they are enlisted in God's army. He is the Lord of Hosts, the Lord of Armies, and the Christian Church is the army of Jesus. When we attack sin, we are either attacking idols outside the church and calling sinners to repentance, or attacking idols inside the church and calling sinners to repentance. While there is a crucial difference between talking to a corpse and talking to a resurrected corpse, the sin is still sin. And the sin is always a crutch or a cover: an attempt at finding safety, security, comfort, peace, meaning in something or someone other than Christ. And almost always, those crutches were snatched up from family, friends, television, celebrities, etc., grasping for what looks safe or what looks cool.

Peter Leithart and I have argued that the book of Job provides a curriculum of sorts for our current generation describing how God loves to grow His people up into maturity—specifically an increasing maturity that learns to stand before God, to speak with Him, and to know Him as a friend. Basically, God is the original Principal of the School of Hard Knocks. God beams over His servant Job . . . and sends the Accuser to trash his life. God beams again with exuberant, fatherly pride . . . and lets the Accuser cover Job's body in boils. God is apparently still beaming as He lets three backstabbing friends show up, complete with Bible verses, showy religious rituals, and a Russian novel's worth of accusations and lies.

Job cries. Job curses. Job explodes in tirades of righteous indignation. Job prays with the vehemence of the Psalmist. He argues. He defends himself. He starts blogging and opens a Twitter account and blasts the media, the tar-and-feather crew outside the royal estate, and all the smear blogs popping up all over the kingdom. The climax is often misunderstood. When God shows up in the whirlwind, this is not a cosmic smackdown. God is glorious and wonderful and transcendent, and Job is a puny ant with a righteous bad attitude. Absolutely. But the thing that most commentators miss is the fact that God has a huge fatherly smile on His face. God is not upset with Job. At the end of the story, God says Job was right (Job 42:7). Job is vindicated. God says that Job threw a holy tantrum, and *well done, my boy, well done*.

The way into the storm-presence of God was through the storm of calamities and enemies and arguments. God is the great fighter, and He runs the universe. God plays with weather systems and in His free time wrestles Leviathan. And as we've seen, Jesus came to fight the demons, and heal the brokenness, and calm the storms, and make peace through the blood of His cross. And like the faithful father that God is, He wants His beloved sons to grow up to rule the universe as He does. He wants His sons to play with dragons too. And so He sends little dragons to attack and tempt and try His beloved sons, so that they can learn to wrestle, fight, and die like Him.

The conflicts, the misunderstandings, the failures, the hard providences are not an accident. The Wind of the storm is the Breath of God hovering over our lives, our communities, our churches, our families, surging, howling, blowing. And apart from Jesus we get scared. We don't want calamities. We want everything to stay peaceful and calm and on the shelf where we left it. But this is impossible, because God is determined to remake this world. God is determined to undo all the brokenness and chase the darkness all away.

But not only do we shrink away from the fights and the danger, it's a generational temptation to get bored with the old battles and to grow apathetic. We don't see the use in fighting. We don't see any apparent progress. We get tired of all the wrangling, all the arguments. *And besides, maybe the other guys have a point after all.* Why enter the fray? Why argue? Does it really accomplish anything? *Look at all the divisions in the church. Look at all the infighting.* Jesus didn't say that we would be known for our denominations, our fragmentation, our blog wars. He said we'd be known for our love for one another. *Great witness, modern church, way to go.* And besides, we'd rather be winsome and irenic. It's easier to be suave and subtle. We'd rather tell stories that disarm and loosen people up. It's hard to disagree with stories, and people don't tend to split churches over novels. Didn't Jesus tell lots of stories? And isn't the gospel all about grace? Jesus said to love our enemies, to turn the other cheek, to do good to all men.

And to be sure, I'm all for graciousness and kindness and generosity, but some folks seem to have gotten the idea that those fruits of the Spirit are *opposed* to the armor of God and the sword of the Spirit and the war that Jesus is currently engaged in *in history*. Jesus gives peace *and* He came to make war. Jesus was cool with saying both things, and so should we. We are warriors and peacemakers, and if you think that's a contradiction, *take it up with Jesus*.

Of course there's some truth to the complaints. Churches dividing over trifles is a bad witness. A church blowing up over the color of the carpet in the foyer is a bad witness . . . but churches actually *don't* blow up "over the color of the carpet in the foyer," no matter what anyone says. That may be the reason given to the newspaper reporter, or what went in the minutes, or what was posted on Facebook, but that's a lie. Churches divide over trivial matters because they are too cowardly to actually deal with the serious problems raging under the surface. The color of the carpet was just the easiest and—ironically—least embarrassing place to throw down. People who love Jesus will refuse to argue about the color of the carpet. The faithful who love Jesus won't strangle gnats because Jesus said not to. And anyway, their hearts are so gripped by the grace of God that such penny-pinching is laughable. But Pharisees are professional gnat stranglers. Pharisees walk around with magnifying glasses and microscopes strapped to their heads, and it's no wonder they leave a trail of strangled gnats and broken people and badly installed carpet in their wake. And when anyone points out the damage they're doing . . . *it's going to get real.*

This is why the Church can be full of millions of professing Christians who can only manage to get in fights about the carpet. The tragedy is not that there are divisions and fights—the tragedy is that there are so many real live enemies all around us, and we're busy scuffling in the baggage train over stupid stuff. Lots of people see the silly scuffling and get all embarrassed about the idea of fighting. Whenever any Christian conflict hits the news, you can bet that some idiot will set up a press conference the next week, and (tugging his collar apologetically) he'll assure all the philistines that we don't actually want anyone to get hurt, and *especially not anyone's feelings.* We're certainly not trying to get anyone too worked up about any ideas or *doctrines.* We're just here to tell cute, sexy stories.

This is a particular travesty when it comes to missions and mercy work. Visiting third-world countries or living in cardboard boxes next to homeless people in the inner city make for fabulously gritty stories. This is a perfect spirituality for a video game generation, for a Reality TV culture, for a people addicted to pornographic orgasms. You can get all the stimulation and release of the real sacrifice without as much trouble, without as much pain, and certainly without all the struggle, fighting, arguments with real live people. And that way, no one has to hear about the real people who were really hurting, really oppressed, and who got used and forgotten in the process.

But I've got a story for you: it's about a Jewish man who claimed to be God and walked into his church one day and started one of the biggest church splits ever. He made people so mad that they eventually killed him, and then most of his followers got killed for proclaiming that he was right and that God had raised him from the dead and offered complete forgiveness of sins to all who trusted in Him. And yes, that message includes love and grace for the lost, the hurting, the broken, the suffering, the lonely, the homeless, the dying. And yes, in so far as American Christians live comfortably without care for the hurting and lonely around them, God damn our selfish arrogance.

Jesus declared war on Pharisees, and anyone who wants to follow Jesus needs to get used to this war. It's not sexy. It's not cool. It won't win you any accolades. You won't be *Time*'s "Man of the Year" or get asked to be on the cover of *GQ*. But Jesus didn't promise that. If you're looking for glamour, go try another religion. If you're looking for silence and solitude and tranquility try something eastern. Jesus said if you follow Him, you're signing up for the messiness of fighting sin and hypocrisy in all its forms. Jesus said that following Him means a cross. And there is no other way. This means that you will get accused of being belligerent. You will get accused of trolling. And then you'll get accused of fighting over semantics. But the response of the children of God, the response of those who have met Jesus and have been conquered by His grace should be something along the lines of: *Yeah, well, bring it.*

The great thing is that ultimately it doesn't matter what anyone thinks if Jesus is pleased with you. If God sends the blessing, then we don't need the blessing of anybody. At the same time, we must be people of compassion and sympathy for real victims who are really hurting. But one of the ways we show compassion for them is by fighting the bad guys who are either inflicting the wounds or healing the wounds lightly (Jer. 6:14). If you knew that some doctors were prescribing medicine for a disease that covered up some of the more obvious symptoms but didn't actually bring healing (and maybe even made things worse), wouldn't you say something?

So in the name of equality, in the name of the hurting, in the name of the poor, many perpetrate great evils. Sometimes this is the refusal to talk about sin, the core cause of all brokenness, addiction, and abuse. Sometimes it's clear that the driving force behind this mercy is some deep ego issue. Who needs whom, exactly? Do you need to be needed? Are you setting captives free or are you perpetuating their codependency by coddling them and manipulating them in the name of justice? People who really care about orphans and widows and addicts and victims should be willing to put their reputations on the line, willing to put their careers on the line, willing to get slurred and slandered and lied about, when wolves break into the fold in the name of mercy and justice.

Because you'll totally get made to look like you're blowing up the Red Cross bus. But Jesus said something somewhere about being slandered.

Let's be absolutely clear: Jesus came for tax collectors and sinners. He came for the blind, the deaf, the lame, the poor, the abused. True religion is to visit orphans and widows in their distress, but don't forget that it is also to keep oneself unspotted from the world (Jas. 1:27). I'm all for mercy ministry, missions, and loving the unlovely, but only in the name of the Jesus who I know, the Jesus who picked fights with passive-aggressive Pharisees, drove money changers out of the temple, and invited enemies to His table. By all means, befriend the prostitutes, the drug addicts, and the homeless. Invite them into your home, love them, serve them, give generously and sacrificially, but only do it in the name of the One who is actually conquering the cause of all that brokenness, the Son who suffered to learn obedience, the Beloved Son—the greater Job—who throws down, who wrestles, who fights, who argues, who crushed the head of the dragon in His own agonizing death for our sins and has inherited glory.

Otherwise, all your ministry, all your polite platitudes, all your deferential excuse-making, is working long hours during the week for the burn unit of the nearby hospital and being a freelance arsonist on the weekends.

We serve the God who is committed to destroying all arson in order to eradicate the need for all burn units. And until the last enemy is destroyed, we are soldiers, warriors, and sons learning to wrestle, struggle, fight, and argue so that we might grow up into maturity—into Jesus. Jesus fought for us. Jesus suffered for us. Jesus stands before God for us. He argues and pleads for us. And this is so that we, by the power of His Spirit, might bring His justice, His goodness, His light to this world.

So this is a call to enter the fray wherever God has placed you. The particular fronts may change. The hottest spots of the battle may shift over the years, but fight we must. Remember, false prophets don't usually dress up like they crashed into a Hot Topic shop. They aren't in permanent Halloween mode (most of them). They go to church, they go to small groups, they have big families, they are pro-life Republicans, they dig Christian education, and they know about Reformed theology. So the followers of Jesus must be vigilant and fearless. We are at war with all idols and the sinful clutches people have on their idols. We insist on describing sin in all of its disgusting vulgarity because Jesus really was flayed alive and suffered hell for that sin. And He really did rise up triumphant over that sin, conquering the curse of death and darkness and putting His enemies under His feet. Some people may call that harsh, but we call it love.

CHAPTER 20

MANALIVE

This is a book for all Christians, for Pharisees, fakers, posers, and liars. This is a book for seekers, for anybody who wants to know who Jesus really is and to follow Him wherever He leads.

So let's say we've connected. Let's imagine God has met you. Jesus has spoken to you through His word. Let's say you are on your knees, and you are crying out to God for grace, for mercy, for courage, for wisdom, for light. You're tired of being half-assed, you're tired of shirking, you're tired of pretending, and you're sick of the shows, sick of the games, disgusted with your sin, determined to chase after the unending glory of Jesus. You want to know Jesus and the power of His resurrection. You want to walk with Him and serve Him all your days. You want His glory to fill the earth. You want to fulfill the Great Commission. You want to see the nations come and present their gifts to the Lamb that was slain. You want to see every knee bow, every tongue confess that Jesus Christ is Lord. You want to see kings kiss the Son and bow in reverent fear. You want to see true reformation and revival. You want the light of the gospel to shine in this dark place. What do you do? How do you walk with Jesus like that?

I want to answer these questions by going back to the very beginning of the human race, to the creation of the first man and the first woman. Because what we are really saying is that we want to be *human* again. We want to be filled with *that* glory again.

In the beginning, God created men and women to bear His image together, but the first lesson in embracing our humanity again is to recognize that this original glory men and women share is asymmetrical. Men and women contribute differently shaped glories to the whole glory of the human race. When the differences are flattened or erased, the image is distorted, because God gives different kinds of glory to men and women. Another way to say this is that God gives different kinds of *strength*. According to the creation pattern, God gives men the duty to be strong, to protect and lead and work the ground (of whatever field they find themselves in). And, according to the same creation pattern, God gives women the duty to be strong to conceive life, nurture life, and adorn life with glory and beauty. In both cases, sacrifice is absolutely necessary.

And the New Testament is painstakingly clear that these creation realities have not been obliterated by the work of Christ but rather they are in the process of being healed and glorified. We see this when Jesus insists on the inherent sanctity of marriage between one man and one woman, and He does so by appealing to the original creation: "from the beginning of the creation God made them male and female" (Mk. 10:6). He also appeals to the *shape* of creation: the man *leaves* his father and mother and the woman *cleaves* to her husband (Mk. 10:7). This doesn't have to become some kind of wooden bludgeon (as some hyper-conservatives are wont to do) for us to receive the plain point that men and women are different, and therefore they enter marriage differently. This doesn't mean that a woman cannot leave home when she's twenty-two, and this doesn't mean that a man can't be a faithful, industrious vertebrate who happens to live and work on the family farm. But it does mean that there are certain masculine traits (that generally resemble "leaving") that inform how he seeks a bride and wins her, and likewise, there are certain feminine traits (that generally resemble "cleaving") that inform how a woman receives and responds to those advances and agrees to a man's proposal.

So what are these masculine and feminine shaped glories? What makes a godly man powerful? What makes a godly woman powerful?

The Bible's straightforward answer is that a man's glory and power is the sacrifice of his strength to love, lead, and protect those around him. A woman's glory and power is the use of her beauty to conceive, nourish, and glorify life all around her.

Beginning with the original creation, we insist that being created male means being called to die first. The first Adam was cut open and a rib was torn from his side for the creation of the woman. The second Adam (Jesus) was pierced in His side, and blood and water flowed for the creation of the new Eve, the Christian Church (Jn. 19:34). Being first and going first is not grounds for some kind of toddler bragging rights.

Going first into a field of land mines is a privilege, but it's perhaps not the privilege you think. Getting to jump on a live grenade to save your comrades is a glory, but it's the glory of *sacrifice*. Being a *man* means you get to die first. A married man is the *head* of his wife, and one of the implications of this title according to the sacrificial rituals of the Old Covenant is that he goes into the fire first for her (Lev. 1:12–13, 15). When he cheerfully and diligently stands between his wife and every threat, he imitates Jesus, and the Bible calls this love.

This is why God requires men to lead in the Church and in the family, and when they lead well in those areas, their leadership is a cumulative blessing in lots of other areas, like politics and business and science and health. This is why the elders and pastors of the Church must be male (1 Tim. 3:1, Tit. 1:6). This is why husbands must assume responsibility for their families (1 Tim. 5:8). Men were made to be strong in *that* way. The glory of men is their strength (Prov. 20:29). It may mean long days, late nights, and early mornings. It may mean the hardships of personal and family life. It may mean the challenges of difficult coworkers, obstinate employers, or evil men. It may mean speaking the truth boldly, clearly, and cheerfully despite what anyone thinks, and despite the ensuing false accusations and slander. It may mean staring demons in the face and taking out the sword of the Spirit and hacking off hands and carving out eye sockets. It may mean taking flack from dear friends. It may mean betrayal, misunderstanding, and bearing the fears and worries of a wife or children. But men are called to bear the brokenness and needs of their people patiently, firmly, and gladly.

When men do this, their schedules fill up, stresses pile on, and difficulties accumulate. It can be easy to feel overwhelmed, tired, and exhausted, like you have nothing left to give. It might even feel like *dying*. And Jesus says that's just about right. You were made for this. You were made to die. You were made to be strong to bear up under these things. You were made to be strong like *that*. It's no accident that Paul urges all the Corinthians to man up like this: "Watch ye, stand fast in the faith, quit you like men, be strong" (1 Cor. 16:13). When men stand up and lead in submission to King Jesus, when men imitate their Savior and bring healing and teaching and food for their people, when they have nothing to save for themselves, nothing to earn for themselves, nothing to prove for themselves, when they are nothing and Jesus is everything, they are freed to lead and love and die well. And their people are always very blessed.

One of the particular places a man must be strong in this way is by honoring his wife as the weaker vessel (1 Pet. 3:8). And we must not miss the fact that when a man honors a woman's weakness with understanding—this is precisely *how* he remembers that she is an heir of grace together with him (1 Pet. 3:8). When a man honors and guards his wife and gladly sacrifices for her and bears her weakness, he is *at that very point* treating her as a co-heir of life together.

Our culture gets this completely backwards and upside-down. Our world demands that women be treated "equally," which always (and necessarily) means that they are treated like men. And that always results in their mistreatment, abuse, and destruction. To treat a hammer and a teacup equally is necessarily to destroy the teacup. But to treat them differently as each has need is to actually give them equal honor. By honoring difference, we lift one another up as co-heirs of the grace of life.

When we demand undifferentiated treatment, we are (ironically) insisting on inequality. Just look around at the fruits of feminism and egalitarianism: Women are *not* more fulfilled, more protected, more honored.

The disastrous effects are all around us in the form of abortion, single mothers, rampant adultery, sexually transmitted diseases, battered wives, sexually abused daughters, etc. Fifty shades of abuse.

Contrary to this dead end strategy for "empowering" women, the Bible calls Christians (and the whole world) to a far more glorious vision of what it means to be made female in the image of God. In one of the most famous passages outlining what a "virtuous woman" is like, the mother of King Lemuel describes a woman who is involved in industry, real estate investment, commerce, textiles, and philanthropy (Prov. 31:1, 10–31). Not only is she a competent business woman, but she does everything for the good and wellbeing of her husband and children. The word repeated several times throughout this description is "strength" (31:17, 25), and the word translated "virtuous" is often translated "mighty" in the Old Testament—and frequently describes the military might of warriors. The point is that when a woman embraces the feminine-shaped glory that God designed her for, she is actually embracing her unique glory and power.

We see this at work in an apparently *liturgical* context when Paul points to the unique calling of women to be child-bearers: "Notwithstanding she shall be saved in childbearing, if they continue in faith and charity and holiness with sobriety" (1 Tim. 2:15). It might seem a bit odd for Paul to bring up motherhood when speaking generically about men and women, and not explicitly about husbands and wives. But Paul's point actually makes sense given the creational context. Just before this verse, Paul appealed to the creational order of Adam and Eve. The garden was the original sanctuary, and that is where the first sin occurred (cf. 1 Tim. 2:13–14). Immediately following that first sin, the solution to sin is promised through the "seed of the woman," and Adam named his wife "Eve" in faith and repentance believing that she would become the "mother of all the living" (Gen. 3:20). Paul does not mean a woman will be saved through childbearing in a crass, materialistic way, as though a barren woman cannot be saved, but rather, he says that together with faith, love, holiness, and self-control, the maternal calling is taken up into God's plan of salvation for the world (e.g., Pss. 8, 127). Or, to put it another way, there is a feminine-shaped faith, love, holiness, and self-control that is uniquely maternal and used by God to bring His salvation to the world. Think of Sarah, Rebekah, Rachel, Jochebed, Rahab, Naomi, Ruth, Hannah,

Elizabeth, and of course, Mary. In this sense, it is absolutely proper to say that, biblically speaking, every woman is created for motherhood. This doesn't mean that every woman will conceive and bear biological children or even have primary care of raising children. The Bible teaches that the unique biology and physiology of a woman's body points to and signifies this deeper and broader reality that applies to every woman without exception.

We see this at work when Peter gives encouragement to women who have disobedient husbands (1 Pet. 3:1), and he goes straight to a woman's unique calling to be beautiful. Woman was created to be the glory of man (Gen. 2:23, 1 Cor. 11:7); this is her power. Peter is not merely giving a woman coping skills; he's charging women to use their God-given power to win disobedient husbands to obedience (1 Pet. 3:1–2). Peter reminds women that their glory and beauty is not limited to external adorning, but flows out of "the hidden person of the heart with the imperishable beauty of a gentle and quiet spirit, which in the sight of God is very precious" (1 Pet. 3:4). And here's where motherhood comes in. Peter says that this is how the holy women of old have always adorned themselves, in submission to their own husbands, as Sarah obeyed

Abraham, whose *daughters* you are, if you do good and do not fear anything (1 Pet. 3:5–6). Peter says that Sarah's embrace of her duty of submissive adornment toward her husband is simultaneously an act of *motherhood* to all who follow her example. What's striking is that for most of Sarah's life she was barren and childless, and (not to put too fine a point on it) *she had no biological daughters*. But Peter holds her up as a supreme example of motherhood. This is because she embraced her calling to be the glory of man, specifically for her, through obedience to her husband. We see a similar pattern emerge as we survey the rest of Scripture: Deborah was a mother in Israel through her political ministry (Judg. 5:7). King Lemuel's mother is enshrined in Proverbs as a mother of all young men seeking wisdom and an excellent wife (Prov. 31:1ff). Paul asks the Romans to greet a man named Rufus and specifically his mother, who had been a mother to him as well (Rom. 16:13).

We have so many weak churches because they are full of so many weak men and women. We have sold our glory for the porridge of respectability in the world's eyes. We are embarrassed of our creational differences, which are the very sources of our unique gifts and power.

The New Testament opens with Jesus the Bridegroom coming to woo His bride, His love, the Church. And it closes with John's Revelation depicting the Marriage Supper of the Lamb, the holy city coming down out of heaven, prepared as a bride adorned for her husband (Rev. 21:1). First comes the Man to live, to love, to lead, and to die. And then comes the Bride receiving, responding, glorifying, and imitating. Let the egalitarians, feminists, homosexuals, and all their ideological dufflepuds shriek in horror at what sounds, as C.S. Lewis would say, "positively medieval" (as though that were so obviously a bad thing). Let the progressive nannies rush in to protect the human race. We will follow Jesus.

LORD OF HOSTS

The story of the Exodus is famous: the burning bush, the plagues, Passover, a pillar of cloud by day and fire by night, the armies of Pharaoh riding hard after the recently freed slaves, followed by a spectacular night crossing of the Red Sea, while an extraordinary storm descended in such a way as to blow the waves of the sea back and make the river bed dry enough for a couple million refugees to cross over. Only there's one significant detail in that retelling that isn't accurate. Pharaoh had no *armies*.

The word for "armies" or "hosts" is *tsabaoth*. It's used six times in the book of Exodus, and it never refers to soldiers of Pharaoh.

It always refers to the children of Israel.

Let that sink in. The story of the Exodus is not merely a rescue story. It is not merely an emancipation story. It's a *conquest* story. We tend to think the king of Egypt is a paranoid despot, greedy and consolidating. But his fear that "there falleth out any war" and they might "join also unto our enemies, and fight against us, and so get them up out of the land" (Exod. 1:10) actually turns out to have been ironic prescience. Yahweh is the "enemy" whom the Pharaoh chose to pick a fight with, and He *did* declare war on Egypt. And Israel was drawn into the fight, joined this enemy of Egypt, and did get them up out of the land.

This reading is hard to accept because the children of Israel do not appear to have exerted much of a threat at all. Armies? What armies? If anything, they are reluctant, cowardly, fickle, even insubordinate *rabble*. After the first meeting with Pharaoh, they openly complain about God's tactics (5:21). Moses protests to God that His plan will never work because "the children of Israel have not hearkened unto me; how then shall Pharaoh hear me?" (6:12) But God is unmoved. The Lord appoints heads of the fathers' houses among the tribes of Israel to whom He had said, "Bring out the children of Israel from the land of Egypt according to their *armies*" (6:26, emphasis mine).

And just in case we think that may have been a one-time poetical flourish, it keeps coming up: The Lord assures Moses that He will speak through him and his brother Aaron, saying, "I will harden Pharaoh's heart, and multiply my signs and my wonders in the land of Egypt. But Pharaoh shall not hearken unto you, that I may lay my hand upon Egypt, and bring forth mine *armies*, and my people the children of Israel out of the land of Egypt by great judgments" (7:3–4). The King James tries to imply some distinction between the armies of the Lord and the children of Israel but there is no such distinction in the Hebrew text. When the Lord gives instructions for the Feast of Unleavened Bread, the point is repeated again: "And ye shall observe the feast of unleavened bread; for in this self same day I have brought your *armies* out of the land of Egypt" (12:17). And again: "And it came to pass at the end of the four hundred and thirty years, even the selfsame day it came to pass, that all the *hosts* of the Lord went out from the land of Egypt . . . And it came to pass the selfsame day, that the Lord did bring the children out of the land of Egypt by their *armies*" (12:41, 51).

But what about Pharaoh's armies? As Pharaoh's heart completely hardens and he realizes what he has done in allowing Israel to leave, he assembles his chariots and captains. "But the Egyptians pursued after them, all the horses and chariots of Pharaoh, and his horsemen, and his army, and overtook them encamping by the sea" (14:9). Only Pharaoh does not actually have an "army." The Hebrew says that he has "strength." Or again the Lord says, "And I, behold, I will harden the hearts of the Egyptians, and they shall follow them: and I will get me honour upon Pharaoh, and upon all his host, upon his chariots, and upon his horsemen" (14:17). And yet, the Hebrew actually says that Pharaoh has chariots and horsemen, but strictly speaking he has no "host." Again, the word is "strength." Only Yahweh has a *host*. Only the Lord has *armies*. Pharaoh has chariots and captains and horsemen and his own strength. But Pharaoh has no armies.

There is a bit more. Remember that one of the repeated parts of the plan at the burning bush is the *plundering* of the Egyptians: "And I will give this people favour in the sight of the Egyptians: and it shall come to pass, that, when ye go, ye shall not go empty: But every woman shall borrow of her neighbor, and her that sojourneth in her house, jewels of silver, and jewels of gold, and raiment: and ye shall put them upon your sons, and upon your daughters; and ye shall spoil the Egyptians" (3:21–22). And this is exactly what happened: "They plundered the Egyptians" (12:36). Not only are the children of Israel the armies of the Lord, His military host, they are also His conquering, plundering host. Israel, on this reading, does not barely escape as a couple million weak and impoverished refugees. Hardly. On this reading, Israel walks out of Egypt a conquering army, a victorious host. They walk out of Egypt not merely free, not merely escaping with their skin, but loaded with plunder, with gold and silver on their sons and daughters.

There are two things that you shouldn't miss. First off, all of this is nothing but pure, insane *grace*. God is the One who fights for Israel (14:14). God did all the bombing runs that left Egypt in shambles. God was the sniper who brought down the firstborn. He is the one who troubled Egypt in the midst of the sea and took off their chariot wheels. God fought for Israel, and then gave the glory for the victory to His people. But this is not just a cute game, like putting a t-shirt on a baby that says "champ." No, God actually insists that the children of Israel *are* His armies. He's not playing. He's not pretending.

Second, it turns out that even though God did the lion's share of the fighting—nevertheless, Israel did have a role to play. They slaughtered lambs. They painted their doorways with blood. They ate unleavened bread and packed their bags. They asked their neighbors for gold and silver. They walked into the midst of the sea on dry ground. Those are unusual battle tactics. It's similar to marching around a city blowing trumpets and shouting, or similar to breaking open six hundred jars filled with torches in the middle of the night. It's similar to sending the choir out in front of the army. It's similar to pouring water on the head of a child, eating bread and drinking wine, and singing the praises of the Triune God at the top of your lungs. Turns out the armies of God have always used *unusual* tactics. Turns out the Lord of Armies has always been pleased to enlist women and children and old men with speech impediments. And what looks irrelevant to the world, what looks silly, weak, and irrelevant is in fact potent in the service of the God of the universe.

This is why Paul says, "who shall separate us from the love of Christ? Shall tribulation, or distress, or persecution, or famine, or nakedness, or peril or sword?" (Rom. 8:35). What if they're killing us all day long, like sheep for the slaughter (v. 36)? Paul says, "Nay, in all these things we are more than conquerors through Him that loved us" (v. 37). *More than conquerors.* Yes, even if we're being killed all day long, Paul smiles and says, now we've got them on the run. Hmm . . . lots of lambs led to slaughter. Remind you of anything? We'll be plundering those poor fools any minute now.

Because of the love of Christ. Because Jesus sets us free from the prison of selfishness, defensiveness, and protectiveness—and all our idols. Because we are covered in His blood, now the Angel of Death cannot touch us with anything. So we aren't afraid of anything or anyone. We laugh at sin and death and shame. "For I am persuaded, that neither death, nor life, nor angels, nor principalities, nor powers, nor things present, nor things to come, nor height, nor depth, nor any other creature, shall be able to separate us from the love of God, which is in Christ Jesus our Lord" (vv. 38–39). Our confidence, our boldness is not in our faith or in our strength. We're a bunch of homeless refugees. We're hungry, barefoot, foolish failures, and guilty sinners, and yet, in His great love and compassion, He has claimed us. He has purchased us with His blood. And by His blood, we have been set apart to be His *armies*. Jesus is the Lord of Hosts, and we are His Hosts.

So this is the sum of it all: We aren't here to prove anything. We aren't here to make up for anything. We're here because we have met Jesus, the God who made us and all things. He died for us and took away all our sins. Now we love Him and hate all evil. We love to talk to Him in prayer. We love to feast in our homes and care for the weak. We rejoice in suffering, and we give generously to all in need. We love to sing the old war songs of the Church. We love to listen to Him, particularly His Word. We have been enlisted in His army through baptism, and we feast with His people at His Table. And the world is before us. What will you do? Where will you explore? What will you confront? Whom will you befriend? Where will you bring healing? What will you create?

We own this place.

It belongs to us.

Jesus bought it with His blood.